United States
Department of
Transportation

Volpe National
Transportation
Systems Center

June 2008

VOLPE center

Tongass National Forest

Transportation System Opportunity Study

Final Report for Hoonah and Wrangell Ranger Districts

Executive Summary

Introduction

Tongass National Forest (NF) is in Southeast Alaska, a region rich in natural and cultural resources, which is currently undergoing significant economic change. This study examines how the existing assets of the Tongass NF's transportation system can be better used to generate economic development opportunities in Southeast Alaska communities and focuses on the Hoonah and Wrangell Ranger Districts within the Tongass NF. The study has been prepared by the U.S. Department of Transportation, Volpe National Transportation Systems Center, via an inter-agency agreement with the U.S. Department of Agriculture Forest Service (USFS), Alaska Region Office.

Recommended project proposals

Initial identification of project proposals was based on a stakeholder-driven process. The goal of involving stakeholders was not only to draw on local knowledge and expertise, but also to lay the groundwork for continuing stakeholder involvement and the fostering of partnership arrangements.

Stakeholders' ideas for transportation-related projects were analyzed along several dimensions, including expected benefits and economic impacts; degree of local support; scope, cost, and complexity; and funding and partnership options. While very few of the identified opportunities were based exclusively on existing transportation facilities, the resulting set of recommended project proposals does reflect the study's focus on leveraging existing assets. The recommendations include:

- **Measures to improve the access and efficiency of the existing transportation network**, including Wrangell wayfinding signage and a Tongass-wide online trip planning website
- **Improvements or expansions of current transportation assets to improve connectivity and recreational options,** including upgrades to the Tsunami Trail, extension of bike trails on Wrangell Island, and formalization of a portage trail on Etolin Island
- **Targeted investments in tourism infrastructure** to support recreational use along the road and maritime transportation networks, including a marine access point and visitor facilities at Freshwater Bay, group shelters on Wrangell Island, facilities to support winter recreation on Wrangell Island, and a study of potential marine access points using reciprocal right-of-way exchanges
- **New and/or improved intermodal access to existing recreational resources**, with a focus on tying together isolated road systems and providing additional recreation and tourism opportunities. Specific concepts include new access to Neka Hot Springs, a land route to Point Adolphus, and new ferry service between Hoonah and Glacier Bay / Gustavus.

Transportation analysis and economic impact

These projects were then analyzed in greater depth to assess the role and adequacy of current transportation assets in achieving these projects; to identify basic implementation options and constraints for any additional facilities needed; and to model expected economic impacts. The transportation analysis provides a basic assessment of viability and cost elements and highlights the steps needed to move from opportunities to implementation. For each project, funding and partnership options and other major next steps along the path to implementation are provided.

The economic analysis is based on a well-established model of visitor spending in gateway communities, and indicates that these projects could produce significant increases in local sales and income, though the impact on overall employment would be relatively minor. In addition to the calculated changes in direct visitor spending and economic impact, these investments would also set the stage for future growth in the visitor economy in these communities by improving the overall attractiveness of the area for independent visitors and by improving prospective visitors' access to local travel information.

Table of Contents

Introduction: Purpose and Scope

The purpose of this study is to examine how the existing assets of the Tongass National Forest's transportation system can be better used to generate economic development opportunities in Southeast Alaska communities, especially those in economic distress. The study has been prepared by the U.S. Department of Transportation, Volpe National Transportation Systems Center (Volpe Center), via an inter-agency agreement with the U.S. Department of Agriculture Forest Service, Alaska Region Office (Forest Service or USFS).

Tongass National Forest (NF) is situated in Southeast Alaska, an area blessed with many natural and cultural resources that is undergoing significant economic change.[1] Many of Southeast Alaska's communities are suffering from economic distress related to the decline of timber and other resource extraction industries. At the same time, tourism has been growing steadily, and there are many examples of communities in the United States and abroad that have used transportation as a catalyst for growth in tourism and recreation, and thus for local economic development. For example, Iceland has used its location as a mid-Atlantic air transportation hub to promote tourism. Other case studies can be found in Appendix A.

From a transportation perspective, one of the premises of the study is that economic and social changes in the Tongass region have affected the uses and economic significance of the forest road system. These roads were developed in the 1970s and 1980s with a primary focus on supporting the timber harvest, evolving as an isolated set of logging roads with connections to tidewater via Log Transfer Facilities. Current use of the road system is not primarily in connection with timber extraction but for community and intra-community access for goods and services, subsistence, access to fishing and hunting, recreation, wildlife viewing and other ecotourism activities.

In addition to its specific research objectives, therefore, this study also identifies new paradigms for transportation planning, and for making use of existing resources, that respond to these changes in usage. Rather than simply a means of harvesting timber, the forest road system can be conceived of as a valuable asset for accessing recreational opportunities and for developing local tourism industries. Many of the projects suggested in this study are new or expanded facilities, but in each case the existing transportation network is the key asset that provides access for recreation and tourist use. One aspect that is of growing importance is the role of partnerships – with municipalities, other federal agencies, and community organizations – to develop and maintain transportation infrastructure and to leverage transportation access in the creation of economic development opportunities.

While the study is intended to cover the entire Tongass NF area, it is being conducted in phases, with emphases on particular Ranger Districts. This report covers the **Hoonah** and **Wrangell** Ranger Districts. For each district, the report identifies a set of tourism and recreation opportunities and presents an initial needs assessment of the transportation-related investments that could be made in order to capitalize on those assets. Two Tongass-wide concepts that emerged from the study are also discussed. The report then summarizes the results of an initial

---

[1] Kline, J., L.E. Kruger, and R. Mazza. "Demographic trends in southeast Alaska." In Mazza, R. and L.E. Kruger, tech. eds., *Social conditions and trends in southeast Alaska*. Gen. Tech. Rep. PNW-GTR-653, September 2005.

round of analysis on the potential economic impacts of these new opportunities for local communities. The concluding section of the report identifies the next steps for analysis and for building partnerships to move toward realization of the projects.

Methodology / Summary of Activity

The initial phase of this study consisted of context-setting research on (1) the socioeconomic profile of Southeast Alaska, and (2) evidence from the literature on the local economic impacts of tourism and recreation, including "lessons learned" from other communities that have attempted to make a transition from a primarily resource-based economy. This research was designed to shed light on pertinent issues and trends and ensure that subsequent analysis was based on a firm empirical foundation. Findings from this research were reported in a project memo in November 2006. The full memo is included here as Appendix A and key findings are briefly summarized below.

Profile of Southeast Alaska

Approximately 73,000 people live in Southeast Alaska, spread out across approximately 29,000 square miles of islands and mainland. The Tongass NF covers about 80 percent of this area, with much of the rest held by other federal and state agencies, or by Alaska Native corporations. Table 1 provides a basic demographic profile of Southeast Alaska and the two largest settlements within the study area.

Table 1: Demographic profile of Southeast Alaska

	United States	Southeast Alaska	City of Hoonah	City of Wrangell
Total Population	281,421,906	73,082	860	2,308
Median Age (Years)	35.3	35.9	35.6	39.1
Female	50.9%	48.6%	47.0%	48.5%
White	75.1%	71.2%	28.7%	73.5%
American Indian or Alaska Native	0.9%	17.1%	60.6%	15.5%
Median household income	$41,994	n.a.	$39,028	$43,250
Persons below poverty level	12.4%	7.6%	16.6%	9.0%
High school graduate or higher	80.4%	90.1%	80.5%	82.2%

Source: US Bureau of the Census, 2000, summary file 3. The Southeast Alaska column comes from Kline, J., L.E. Kruger, and R. Mazza. "Demographic trends in southeast Alaska." In Mazza, R. and L.E. Kruger, tech. eds., *Social conditions and trends in southeast Alaska*. Gen. Tech. Rep. PNW-GTR-653.

For many decades, the economy of Southeast has been based primarily on a mixture of resource extraction industries – timber, mining, and fishing – and related manufacturing and processing. Public administration has also been an important component, due in part to the presence of the Forest Service and the many state offices in the capital city of Juneau. Timber production has dropped substantially since 1990 due to a number of factors, including changes in market conditions, revisions to public land management policies, and unfavorable movements in foreign currency exchange rates. During the period from 1990 to 2000, the annual timber harvest from the Tongass National Forest fell from 470 million board feet (mmbf) to 120 mmbf[2]. Other industries related to natural resources have held slightly more steady, but face challenges of their own. For example, the fishing industry is dealing with declining market share for wild Alaskan salmon, the effects of competition from farmed salmon produced in other regions, and the need to regulate local fish stocks[3].

One of the few bright spots in the local economic picture has been tourism. During the period from 1990 to 2005, the number of cruise-based visitors to Juneau (a proxy for the Southeast as a whole) rose from approximately 237,000 to over 949,000, the equivalent of over 9 percent annual average growth. Independent (non-cruise) visitation also appears to be on the rise, although data are more limited. Tourism and related industries are estimated to contribute $250 million per year to Southeast Alaska's economy[4]. This includes visitor spending at the relatively new Icy Strait Point area just outside of Hoonah, a growing destination for cruise ships that was developed by the Huna Totem Corporation.

Stakeholder Consultation

The transportation concepts that are analyzed in this study are primarily the result of an extensive consultation process that assessed the views and priorities of local stakeholders regarding recreation and tourism options and the associated transportation investments. The focus on stakeholders' own ideas and concepts was an outgrowth of two realities. First, in the current fiscal environment, many sources of transportation funding place a premium on projects that are based on partnerships and that reflect a strong degree of local support. Second, the rapid growth in tourism in Southeast Alaska has created a wide range of opinions, both within and across communities, on the effects of tourism and the desirability of further growth. It is important that these opinions be understood and that the concepts pursued reflect community values.

Stakeholders were defined as those individuals and organizations with an identifiable interest in recreational use of the Tongass transportation system in the Hoonah and Wrangell Ranger Districts. This includes internal USFS stakeholders as well as local governments, Tribal organizations, transportation providers, the local tourism and hospitality industry, community organizations, other road users, and advocacy groups. Specific names and contact information were provided by the Hoonah and Wrangell Rangers and their staff, and additional stakeholders were identified as the project proceeded.

The first stage of the consultation process consisted of semi-structured telephone interviews based on the discussion guide shown in Appendix B. The purpose of the interviews was to obtain information on local resources and attractions, visitation patterns, transportation needs, community priorities, existing plans and projects, and constraints. Wherever possible, these initial contacts were followed up with personal interviews during a site visit to the Hoonah and

---

[2] Southeast Alaska Comprehensive Economic Development Strategy. Prepared for the US Department of Commerce by the Southeast Conference and Central Council Tlingit and Haida Indian Tribes of Alaska, April 2001.
[3] Ibid.
[4] Dugan, Darcy. "The Economic Contribution of Southeast Alaska's Nature Based Tourism," Institute of Social and Economic Research, University of Alaska, 2006.

Wrangell districts during the week of June 25, 2007. The site visit also included many of the sites and transportation facilities being studied. All told, the following stakeholders took part in the consultation process:

- Julianne Baltar, SE Tribal Department of Transportation / Central Council Tlingit & Haida (Telephone)
- Bob Barton, Forget-Me-Not Outfitters, Hoonah (Telephone & Personal)
- Erica Bjorm, Southeast Alaska Conservation Council (Telephone)
- Odin Brudie, Alaska Department of Commerce, Community, and Economic Development – Office of Economic Development (Personal)
- Andrei Chakine, Central Council Tlingit & Haida (Personal)
- Dennis Chapman, Museum Director, James & Elsie Nolan Center, Wrangell (Personal)
- Jackie Dick, Hoonah Economic Development Committee (Telephone)
- Johanna Dybdahl, Tribal Coordinator, Hoonah Indian Association (Personal)
- Dan Fanning, D&L Woodworks, Hoonah (Telephone)
- Dennis Gray, Mayor, City of Hoonah (Telephone & Personal)
- Bruce Harding, Sourdough Lodge, Wrangell (Telephone & Informal Personal)
- Tyler Hickman, Vice President for Operations and Site Director, Icy Strait Point (Telephone & Personal)
- Wayne Howell, Gustavus City Council / Glacier Bay NP (Telephone)
- Carl Johnson, Director of Public Works and Capital Projects, City of Wrangell (Personal)
- Amber King, SEAtrails (Personal)
- Len Laurence , Mariner Inc., Ketchikan – marketing contractor to Inter-Island Ferry Authority (Telephone)
- Cliff Lobaugh, Sierra Club Juneau Group (Telephone)
- Sandy Marchbanks, Mayor, City of Gustavus (Telephone)
- Marie Obozcky, Rain Walker Expeditions / Wrangell Convention and Visitors Bureau (Telephone & Personal)
- Patricia Phillips, Mayor, City of Pelican (Personal)
- Terree Pino, Muskeg Meadows Golf Course, Wrangell (Personal)
- Janelle Privett, Wrangell Chamber of Commerce (Telephone & Personal)
- Steve Prysunka, Director, Wilderness Programming, Alaska Crossings, Wrangell (Telephone & Personal)
- Carol Rushmore, Economic Development Department, City of Wrangell (Telephone)
- Gabriel Scott, Cascadia Wildlands Project (Attempted)
- Keith Skaflestad, Outfitter & Guide, Hoonah (Personal)
- Wilma Stokes, Wrangell Cooperative Association (Telephone)
- Andrew Thoms, Sitka Conservation Society (Telephone)
- Wes Tyler, Icy Strait Lumber, Hoonah (Telephone)
- Steven Wade, Economic Development Specialist, Central Council Tlingit & Haida (Telephone & Personal)
- Lee Wallace, Transport Planner, Wrangell Cooperative Association (Telephone)
- Liana Wallace, Central Council Tlingit & Haida (Attempted)
- Patrick Wickens, Guide / Hoonah Economic Development Committee (Personal)
- Bob Wysocki, President and CEO, Huna Totem Corporation (Personal)
- Eric Yancey, Breakaway Adventures, Wrangell (Telephone)

In November 2007, this group was contacted again by mail with an update on the project and a list of all of the recreation, tourism, and related concepts that had been suggested by stakeholders during the interviews and given the opportunity to comment on the concepts. This "long list" is included as Appendix C. It included a diverse mix of suggestions, including:

- Small-scale local projects, such as improvements to existing trails
- More ambitious regional concepts, such as new ferry routes
- Complex infrastructure projects (e.g. Bradfield Road connection to Canada)
- Ideas for related tourism infrastructure, such as shelters, wayfinding signage, cabins, and expanded local accommodation
- Concepts for partnerships and coordination with other ongoing planning processes and related groups (e.g. with SEAtrails and Central Council Tlingit and Haida)
- New government approaches or entities (e.g., a new borough government)
- Alternative visions of local economic development, such as investing in telecommunications to promote tele-work and tele-medicine.

In reviewing this list of stakeholder suggestions, it was clear that certain concepts could not be analyzed at this point because they are beyond the scope of the current study – for example, those that were not closely related to the transportation system or to recreation and tourism. In other cases, the proposed projects are being studied as part of other planning processes, and are not included here to avoid duplication of effort. Moving from the long list to a short list of potential high-value projects that would warrant further analysis also required a review of existing plans and research. The studies and documents reviewed included the following:

- Hoonah Ranger District, Recreation Master Plan (2004, revised 2006)
- Hoonah Ranger District, Access and Travel Management Plan Environmental Assessment (2001)
- Hoonah Ranger District, Decision Memo, Neka Hot Springs Trail & Hot Tub (2001)
- Wrangell Ranger District, Access and Travel Management Plan Environmental Assessment (2007)
- Wrangell Downtown Revitalization Plan: Final Report, Jones & Jones Architects and Landscape Architects for City of Wrangell, (2006)
- Southeast Alaska Comprehensive Economic Development Strategy, Southeast Conference and Central Council Tlingit and Haida Indian Tribes of Alaska (2006)
- State Transportation Improvement Plan, 2006-2008, and Southeast Alaska Transportation Plan, Alaska Department of Transportation & Public Facilities (2004)
- SEAtrails Trail and Transportation Master Plan (2005)
- Tongass National Forest, Forest Level Roads Analysis, Foster Wheeler Environmental Corporation for USFS (2003)
- Federal transportation law, in particular Public Law 109-59, Section 4407 on reciprocal rights-of-way.

Based on the stakeholder process and review of documentation, a "short list" of potential projects was produced using the following selection criteria:

- User and non-user benefits,
- Extent of local support,
- Scope and complexity of the project,
- Likelihood of developing partnerships and/or obtaining external funding,
- Relationship to other (ongoing or planned) projects and initiatives,
- Lifecycle and maintenance costs, and
- Expected economic impact.

In the sections that follow, a set of recommended projects and concepts are discussed for each Ranger District, in addition to two Tongass-wide concepts that also emerged favorably from the stakeholder process. Each section presents background information on the Ranger District and a summary of the proposed concepts. The concepts are then analyzed along their *transportation* and *economic* dimensions. The transportation analysis describes the components of the project, construction options and constraints, and initial components of a cost estimate. For longer-term and larger-scale projects, the transportation analysis focuses on identifying potential concepts of operation and the next steps for further data collection and analysis. A summary of the transportation impacts is provided in Table 2. The economic analysis is based on a model of local impacts of visitation and tourism. Using a baseline of current tourism-related expenditures in the Tongass area, the model quantifies the potential local economic impacts of increases in visitation associated with the proposed improvements.

Analysis of Proposals – Hoonah Ranger District

The Hoonah Ranger District

The Hoonah Ranger District is located in the northern section of the Tongass NF, covering approximately 1,036 square miles, principally on Chichagof and Yakobi Islands. The largest settlement in the area is Hoonah, a city of about 860 residents that is the primary home of the Huna Tlingit tribe. Pelican, Elfin Cove, and Tenakee Springs are smaller communities that are in or adjacent to the District. Of these, Pelican and Elfin Cove are fishing-oriented villages while Tenakee Springs is largely a retirement and resort community[5].

As with other communities in Southeast Alaska, the city of Hoonah has experienced economic distress due to downturns in the timber and fishing industries. The unemployment rate is around 20 percent[6]. However, tourism to Hoonah has been growing rapidly in the past few years. At Point Sophia, just over a mile from downtown, the Huna Totem Corporation has re-developed a 1912 former salmon cannery as Icy Strait Point, a destination for several major cruise lines. Icy Strait Point had its first full season in 2004. During the 2007 season, 81 large cruise ships (about 5 per week) called at Icy Strait and 137 people (almost all local) were employed at the facility[7].

Figure 1: Icy Strait Point, Hoonah, AK

---

[5] Alaska DCED, Alaska Community Database Community Information Summaries.
[6] US Bureau of the Census, 2000, summary file 3.

Icy Strait Point has museum exhibits about Huna Tlingit culture and a display of historic cannery operations, as well as several shops and restaurants. It serves as a launching point for shore excursions that include a new zipline, a tour of Hoonah, bike tours, charter fishing, ATV tours, seafood dinners, wilderness tours, and wildlife exploration. Because Hoonah is less intensely commercialized than other ports of call, it is not uncommon for cruise visitors to describe it as their opportunity to see the "real Alaska," or even to make plans to return to Hoonah and spend time there as an independent traveler[8].

This exposure has contributed to Hoonah's growing reputation as a unique and interesting place to visit, with a mix of cultural activities and opportunities for wildlife observation and outdoor recreation. The local community is interested in fostering more independent tourism, which would complement the existing cruise-oriented market and provide some needed diversification in the local hospitality industry. As others have noted, independent visitors often also yield more local economic impact, because they pay more for local accommodation and meals and the income produced is more likely to stay in the local community.[9] (Independent tourists also use the Alaska Marine Highway System, which helps to shore up the financial viability of this transportation system, which is crucial for local and regional mobility.)

Local attitudes toward tourism are still evolving. There is local interest in ensuring that visitors not confine themselves to Icy Strait Point but also come downtown so that the larger community can benefit economically. However, this is balanced by continuing reticence about the effects of large-scale tourism on the local way of life[10]. In light of these concerns – and, perhaps more to the point, to preserve the quality of the visitor experience – Huna Totem has strictly limited cruise ship calls to Icy Strait to no more than one per day, and generally no more than 5 or 6 per week. This means that growth in cruise-based visitation will be modest and reinforces the importance of independent visitors.

The Hoonah Ranger District's road system includes a network of 130 miles of Forest Service roads that connect Hoonah with the Whitestone Logging Camp, Freshwater Bay, Tenakee Inlet, and other points on Chichagof Island. There are also a number of smaller, isolated road systems. These roads were developed primarily for access to timber, but their usage has evolved significantly over time[11]. The roads are now used extensively by local residents for basic mobility and for a wide variety of other purposes, including access to subsistence hunting and berry-gathering areas, picnics and recreation, and even

---

[7] Interviews with Bob Wysocki, Huna Totem, 6-25-07 and Tyler Hickman, Icy Strait Point, 6-29-07.
[8] Interview with Johanna Dybdahl, HIA, 6-30-07.
[9] See, for example, Cerveny, Lee K. *Socioeconomic effects of tourism in Hoonah, Alaska.* Pacific Northwest Research Station, USDA Forest Service, Report PNW-GTR-734, October 2007, and the *Trail and Transportation Master Plan*, prepared by Land Design North for Southeast Alaska Trail System (SEAtrails), May 2005.
[10] Cerveny, Lee K. Socioeconomic effects of tourism in Hoonah, Alaska. Pacific Northwest Research Station, USDA Forest Service, Report PNW-GTR-734, October 2007.
[11] Hoonah Ranger District, Access and Travel Management Plan, Environmental Assessment.

just driving for pleasure. Local outfitters and guides also use the road system for eco-tours, wildlife observation, and related activities. There is interest within the community in seeing greater recreational and tourist use of the Forest beyond the City of Hoonah, which would limit any perceived negative impacts in town.

Hoonah Ranger District Concept

Both local stakeholders and regional groups such as SEAtrails have noted that Hoonah's relative abundance of inter-connected roads – and the superb recreational opportunities to which they provide access – represent great potential for tourism and recreation development. To capitalize on Hoonah's existing assets by linking to nearby attractions and making Hoonah even more of a hub of activity for independent travelers, the study developed the following concept: promote Hoonah as a local transportation hub for nearby attractions, and invest in near-term trail improvements. The concept includes a mix of longer- and shorter-term projects.

Larger / longer-term projects:

Two longer-term projects are included in the concept: improving access from Hoonah to the Neka Hot Springs and/or Point Adolphus and creating a new ferry service between Hoonah and Glacier Bay/Gustavus. Each of these projects is sufficiently complex that the initial stages would consist of environmental and engineering scoping work, review of existing documentation, and analysis of financial and operational viability. Funding for these planning activities could potentially come from the Alternative Transportation in Parks and Public Lands (ATPPL) program (planning category), Transportation Enhancements, and/or local and private funds.

Hoonah to the Neka Hot Springs and/or Point Adolphus
Overview - This project envisions the development of intermodal connections between Hoonah and two major attractions in the vicinity: Point Adolphus, which is a popular site for kayaking and an internationally premier destination for marine mammal observation, and the Neka Hot Springs, a USFS recreation site featuring a natural spring-fed hot tub and a walking trail. Existing Road 8580 provides access to Neka, but this road is not connected to the Hoonah road system. The road also ends 5-10 miles short of the northern shoreline of Chichagof Island and Point Adolphus (see Map 1). As such, there is no land route from the City of Hoonah to these two nearby recreational attractions, and visitors must make all or part of the trip by kayak, skiff, or other private water transport. Indeed, most visitors to Point Adolphus come from the other side of Icy Strait, which represents something of a missed opportunity for Hoonah[12]. This is particularly true since these sites attract independent visitors, with Point Adolphus in particular a major hub for upscale kayak and nature tours. Improving access between these areas and Hoonah would lead to increased visitation and would help to draw at least some visitors into using Hoonah as their base. Gustavus would remain a logical choice for these tours,

---

[12] An online search of whale-watching and kayak tours to Point Adolphus showed that almost all used Gustavus as their starting point (though at least one uses Hoonah).

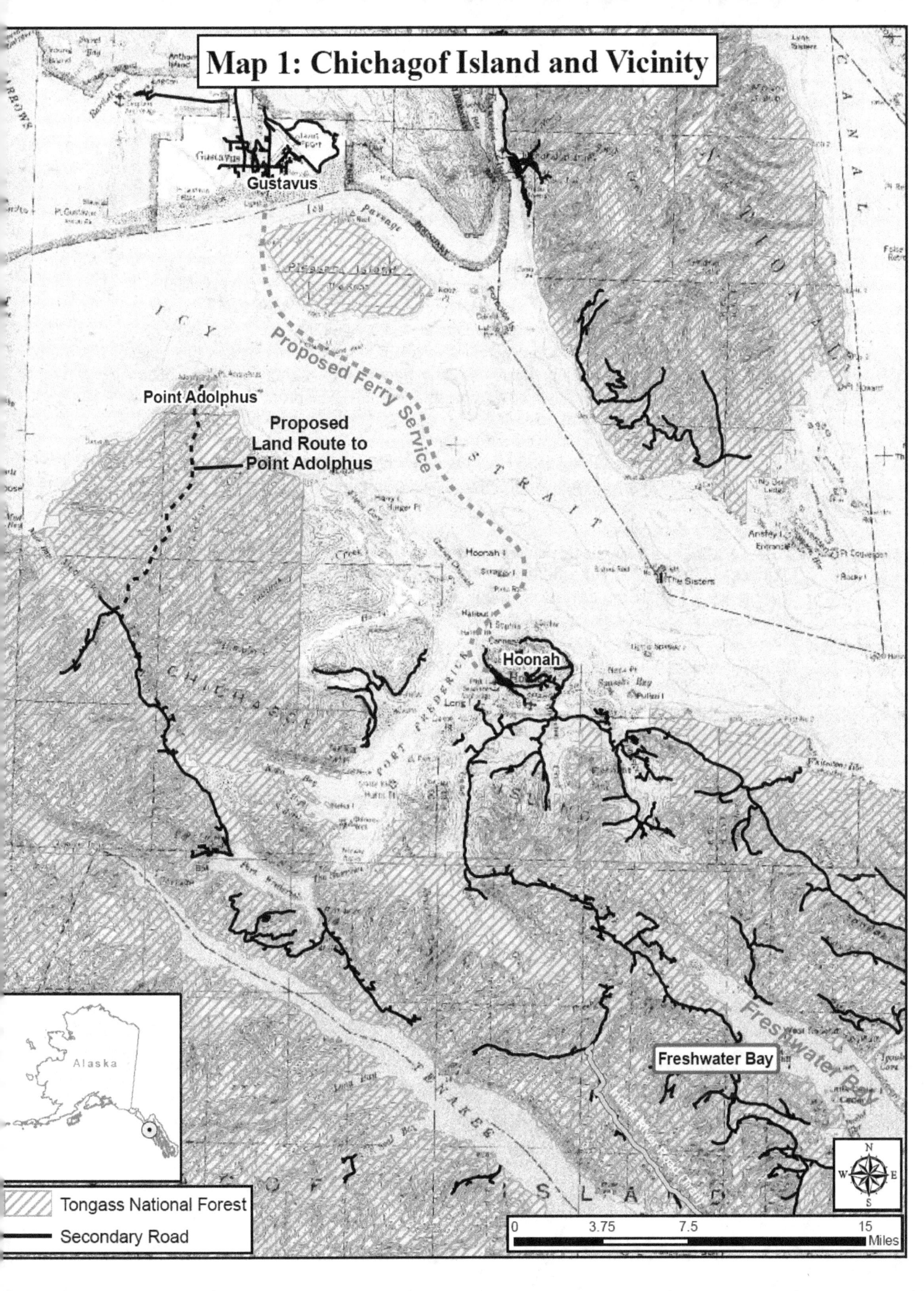

Map 1: Chichagof Island and Vicinity

Gustavus

Point Adolphus

Proposed Land Route to Point Adolphus

Proposed Ferry Service

Hoonah

Freshwater Bay

Alaska

⬡ Tongass National Forest

▬ Secondary Road

0   3.75   7.5   15
Miles

N
W E
S

since it is accessible via seasonal jet service and has a much wider range of commercial accommodation, but it is likely that at least some visitors would be drawn to Hoonah for its unique heritage and attractions.

The number of cruise ship calls to Icy Strait Point has increased in recent years and the number of outfitters/tour guides seeking special use permits to guide cruise ship passengers onto National Forest lands is expected to continue to increase. While the current focus is on areas along the Hoonah road system, prime recreational attractions such as at Point Adolphus and the Neka Hot Springs would be valuable additions to outfitters' offerings. At present, lack of convenient access inhibits local residents and independent visitors based at Hoonah from visiting these recreational sites. This project proposes to improve access to both sites, which could increase visitor stays in Hoonah and allow Hoonah to function as a new transportation hub. The proposal consists of two elements that could be pursued in series or in concert: (1) an intermodal connection between Hoonah and Neka that would effectively link two existing roads, and (2) extension of the existing Road 8580 by a few miles to provide overland access to the recreational attractions of Point Adolphus, thus leveraging the value of the existing road segment.

There are major environmental and engineering constraints on these routes, particularly with extending the road toward Point Adolphus. However, the access routes envisioned for these projects are not necessarily traditional road projects. Options include ATV trails, mountain bike trails, scheduled or on-demand water taxi service, or combinations thereof. Subsequent analysis will also need to take account of the potential ramifications from the state DOT's plans to connect the Hoonah and Tenakee Springs road systems. The strong local opposition to this project within Tenakee Springs makes it difficult to judge the likely impacts, but does suggest at least the possibility of thematic tourism marketing centered on hot springs, as has been the case in Iceland.

Project Elements – A full alternatives analysis would be required to finalize a specific preferred approach, but components could include the following:

- Improvement and expansion of the docks at Port Frederick to support docking of a larger size vessel operated by an outfitter (possibly via concession arrangement with USFS) between Hoonah and Port Frederick. Dock improvements at Hoonah may also be needed.
- Operation of a seamless transport service to Neka Hot Springs, consisting of ferry service to Port Frederick, then onward travel for eight miles on Roads 8577 and 8580. Options examined included motorized and non-motorized ATVs, pedi-cabs, and motor vehicles (e.g. minivan). The ultimate choice of vehicle will depend on trade-offs among factors including ecological impact, protection from bears and other wildlife, visitor preferences, and concession viability.
- Construction of a small parking pull-out at the junction of Road 8580 and the 400-foot boardwalk to Neka Springs. The guided tour would walk the 400 feet to Neka Springs, since the boardwalk has universal access design.

Continuing service from Neka to Point Adolphus would be provided by the concessionaire outfitter as an additional tour option and the route would also be available for use by the kayaking and whale-watching tour groups that are currently based out of Gustavus. Depending on the choice of vehicle, the cross-section of the road extension could be minimized in order to limit environmental impact and construction costs.

Development Feasibility Criteria – The complexity of the project and the lack of consensus on precisely how an overland transportation route serving both Neka Hot Springs and Point Adolphus would be implemented suggests a degree of uncertainty on whether geo-technical, hydrological or other engineering problems make this project technically unfeasible. The proposed concept for a seamless transport service using a multi-modal approach operated by a concessionaire outfitter, and making use of existing infrastructure to the maximum extent, has been suggested as a means of mitigating potential technical and economic risk with the project. Nonetheless, a site survey and reconnaissance are needed to ensure the viability of even a low-impact, unpaved trail connecting Neka with Point Adolphus. Provided the proposed concessionaire outfitter provides the seamless transport service on a group tour basis, at sustainable fares, the USFS commitment for infrastructure improvements (i.e., dock modifications/expansion; parking pull-out; and low-impact narrow trail to Point Adolphus) along the lines suggested under *Project Elements* may be high but acceptable. The project does serve several transportation needs in that it provides access and connectivity to recreational sites that are not currently easily accessible from Hoonah, it lowers user costs and adds convenience to visitors choosing to stay in Hoonah, and it provides social benefits by connecting isolated population to recreational activities.

Cost Elements – For the same reasons that make it difficult to determine technical feasibility, it is not possible to arrive at even a rough cost estimate at this point. For the *Project Element* suggestions articulated above (assuming this is the preferred approach), trail development costs (i.e., site surveying, clearing and grubbing, compaction and grading, drainage structures and bridges required, and any fill needed) could be expected to exceed $250,000 per mile based on recent USFS experience, plus costs for a review process under the National Environmental Policy Act (NEPA) and other compliance activities. Again, however, the proposed design concept is intended to minimize cross-section and functional requirements, and thus costs.

New ferry service between Hoonah and Glacier Bay / Gustavus
Overview - Glacier Bay National Park is one of the most heavily visited areas in the area. In 2006, it recorded just over 413,000 recreation visits, representing nearly 4 in 10 visitors to the Southeast region. The concept of new ferry service across Icy Strait (see Map 1) would help to encourage visitors at Glacier Bay to take a day-trip (or longer, if more accommodation options were available) to Hoonah, where they could explore local culture in town, pursue recreational opportunities along the road system, and/or partake of the many activities that are offered (primarily, but not exclusively, for cruise ship passengers) at the Icy Strait Point facility. The proposed ferry connection would also improve the Huna Tlingit community's access to its original homeland, which is a

priority for the Hoonah Indian Association. As with the Neka and Point Adolphus access proposals above, the goal is to help the Hoonah community capitalize on the assets in its "backyard."

In this case, water transportation is envisioned as a "bridge" connecting the two road systems on either side of Icy Strait. The proposed service makes use of the existing assets of the Hoonah road system, in that visitors coming from Glacier Bay could conceivably access not only downtown Hoonah, but also miles and miles of roads leading into the national forest for wildlife observation or other recreational activities, yet still be back in town by evening for a return ferry. Achieving this vision would also require coordinating suitable ground transportation in Hoonah, which currently has neither a car rental franchise nor public transportation. The increasing number of guided tours and outfitters in Hoonah, as well as the tours organized by the Icy Strait Point cruise facility, suggests that the local tourism industry may be able to fill at least part of this gap. Options for more independent exploration could also be pursued.

This proposed ferry service could also improve overall access to Hoonah for visitors (and local residents) by tying Hoonah more closely to seasonal jet service available at Gustavus. Again, this would also likely require increased connecting transportation (e.g. taxis, shuttle bus) between the dock and airport at Gustavus.

The Huna Totem Corporation is a candidate for potential partnership, as it has a financial interest both in generating more visitor traffic to its facility at Icy Strait Point and in encouraging visitors to spend extra nights at the Glacier Bay lodge that it jointly operates. The City of Gustavus and National Park Service would also be included in partnership discussions, and scenarios would need to take account of the progress of the dock project at Gustavus.

Project Elements – Component elements involve establishing new ferry service connecting Hoonah via the Icy Strait to Gustavus, the gateway to Glacier Bay National Park, and/or to the Park itself. In its most ambitious form, it is a complex project involving not only new service with implications for vessel requirements and crewing, but also adequate facilities to service and maintain the vessels and possibly house the crew and appropriate land-side and docking facilities for passenger handling and intermodal connections at both termini (e.g., ticketing, wayfinding signage system and parking facilities). This analysis is based on a smaller-scale project making use of a chartered vessel and existing port facilities.

Development Feasibility Criteria – Although there are no known engineering problems that make this project technically unfeasible, it would be incumbent to study currents, tides, and bathymetry, as well as migratory fish patterns and sensitive fauna along the shorelines, in order to lay out the precise route and identify any operational constraints.

The project does serve several transportation needs: it provides access and connectivity to visitor attractions and to natural areas not otherwise easily accessible (i.e. via the Hoonah road system); it provides an intermodal connection (a water bridge connecting two landside transport systems otherwise isolated); it provides added comfort, convenience, and lowers user costs; and provides access to ancestral lands for the Huna Tlingit population resident at Hoonah.

Cost Elements – Initial estimates of ferry service costs, ridership, and fare levels were generated using the Volpe Center's ferry cost model. Because this ferry service is still at the conceptual stage, with important details still to be determined, the analysis requires a number of simplifying assumptions. Results should be considered preliminary, but they do provide some insight into the overall viability of the service.

The Volpe Center ferry cost model was used to calculate costs directly attributable to a Hoonah-Gustavus service scenario, including fuel and crew labor, plus an allocated share of indirect costs, such as debt service, maintenance, and insurance. The model allocates indirect costs based on the vessel's operating time on this Hoonah-Gustavus route as a share of its total assumed annual operating time. This allocation assumes the use of a local chartered vessel that operates in other service (e.g. whale-watching) on other days.[13]

All cost inputs were accelerated from those used for a recent New York Harbor analysis to account for economy-wide price increases (particularly for gasoline and marine diesel) and higher costs prevailing in Alaska. The model assumes the availability of public dock facilities in Hoonah and Gustavus, and for simplicity is based on a Hoonah-Gustavus round-trip with no service into Glacier Bay National Park itself.

Boat Options

Two conventional monohull passenger boats were analyzed. Alaska service conditions are demanding in terms of weather, sea conditions, and navigational hazards, all of which militate against the use of a catamaran ferry. The recent difficult experience of the Alaska Marine Highway with a large catamaran ferry was instructive. More to the point, there is little need for a catamaran's speed on this 25-mile run; recreational passengers may indeed prefer the slower pace for sightseeing and watching wildlife.

The model assumes the use of a 15-year-old boat that is in relatively good condition. The specific vessel types analyzed were monohulls with capacities of 49 and 102 passengers and service speeds of 16 and 20 knots, respectively. One-way trip times are in the range of 1½ to 2 hours, which is acceptable for day-trip excursion services of this type.

Ridership and Revenues

According to the National Park Service, in 2006 there were 413,382 visitors to Glacier Bay, but the vast majority of these were based on a cruise ship. The pool of visitors likely to use this ferry service are those staying overnight at Glacier Bay (approximately 5,000 per season[14]) plus those staying outside the park boundaries in Gustavus

---

[13] To be conservative, it is further assumed that the vessel remains in Alaska during the winter and does not operate. Operating the boat year-round, for example by operating in California during the winter, would reduce the allocated share of indirect costs, thus improving the financial viability of the ferry service.

[14] Visitors either staying in concessionaire lodging or camping within Glacier Bay NP.

(approximately 30,000 according to data from the Alaska Visitor Statistics Program). Independent visitors to Hoonah and Hoonah residents may also make use of the service.

Using the ferry model, ridership and revenues were estimated using a number of simple assumptions, including a 14-week peak season, 10-week shoulder season, a 5 percent capture rate among non-cruise overnight visitors to Glacier Bay, Gustavus, and Hoonah, plus local ridership equivalent to one round-trip per season for every four permanent Hoonah residents. It was further assumed that a 50 percent fare discount would be offered to Hoonah residents, and that revenues would include onboard sales of refreshments and souvenirs.

A range of service scenarios were tested, including two or four round-trips during peak season and a combination of peak- and shoulder-season service. Ridership estimates assume that more frequent service (4 round-trips per week) would yield a small amount of induced travel (2 percent over baseline levels),

Model Results

Initial results (details in table below) indicate that the smaller boat clearly makes sense for the projected ridership levels. It also burns less than half the fuel, partly due to its lower speed, though labor costs are slightly higher because of the longer trip times. Break-even fares are quite reasonable in all scenarios, particularly for the smaller boat where they range from $22 to $27 roundtrip depending on the frequency of service. Even with an additional 10 to 20 percent profit margin and further adjustments for higher local price levels and/or fuel price increases, the required fare is well within the typical range for tourist excursions in Southeast Alaska and is roughly comparable (on a per-mile basis) to the passenger fares on the Alaska Marine Highway System and private ferries.

Summary Table: Ferry Cost Model Results for Hoonah-Gustavus Service Concepts

Cost Elements	Scenario 1 Peak Season, 2 round trips per week		Scenario 2 Peak Season, 4 round trips per week		Scenario 3 Peak Season, 4 round trips per week; shoulder season, 2 trips per week	
	Monohull T boat, Capacity: 102 Passengers	Monohull T boat, Capacity: 49 Passengers	Monohull T boat, Capacity: 102 Passengers	Monohull T boat, Capacity: 49 Passengers	Monohull T boat, Capacity: 102 Passengers	Monohull T boat, Capacity: 49 Passengers
Total Round Trips	28	28	56	56	76	76
Total Operating Hours	88	105	176	211	239	286
Boat(s)	1	1	1	1	1	1
Crew (per boat)	3	3	3	3	3	3
Consumables (fuel, lubricant)	$27,062	$12,458	$54,125	$24,915	$73,455	$33,813
Labor, boat crews	$10,749	$12,850	$21,499	$25,700	$29,177	$34,879
Allocated Vessel maintenance	$2,879	$2,095	$5,757	$4,187	$7,911	$5,670
Allocated insurance	$1,460	$1,040	$2,920	$2,077	$4,053	$2,808
Allocated debt service	$5,914	$4,212	$11,826	$8,414	$16,416	$11,372
TOTAL OPER. COST	$48,064	$32,655	$96,125	$65,295	$131,012	$88,542
OPERATING COST / HR.	$545	$310	$545	$310	$547	$309
Revenue						
Ridership						
Tourists						
Gustavus-Hoonah	1,400	1,400	1,960	1,960	2,310	2,310
Hoonah-Gustavus	400	400	560	560	660	660
Hoonah residents	215	215	215	215	301	301
Onboard sales ($10/tourist)	$18,000	$18,000	$25,200	$25,200	$29,700	$29,700
Breakeven RT fares						
Tourists	$20	$10	$34	$19	$41	$24
Residents	$10	$5	$17	$10	$20	$12

Smaller / Near-term projects

This concept for Hoonah also includes some smaller, near-term trail and recreation amenity improvements that would also serve to improve the environment for independent tourism in the study area. These include the Tsunami Trail in Pelican and Freshwater Bay improvements on Chichagof Island.

Pelican: Tsunami Trail

Overview - This project is a trail that has been recognized as a valuable asset in need of formalization and improvements. For the city of Pelican, the Tsunami Trail is both a recreational resource (e.g. for overnight visitors who are looking for a place to hike) and a means of emergency evacuation in the case of a tsunami warning in the Pacific. The trail runs for approximately one-half mile, starting at the southern end of town (Pelican Flats) and rising steeply through forest into an area of muskeg (see Map 2). The Tsunami Trail is a narrow dirt path in fairly primitive condition. It passes through rough terrain and is crossed in several places by small streams. The mayor of Pelican has identified improvements to the trail as a top priority. Specific improvements could include:
- Re-surfacing the trail with a firmer and more stable surface
- Widening the trail from single person width to accommodate 2-3 people walking abreast
- Adding small bridges at the stream crossings
- Adding interpretive signage about flora and fauna.

These improvements would increase the recreation potential of the trail as well as its effectiveness in an emergency evacuation. Upgrades to the trail would also lay the groundwork for an eventual expansion of the trail into a four-mile loop around Pelican, as envisioned by SEAtrails and other local recreation groups. As such, the trail improvements would be a strong candidate for funding through a partnership with City of Pelican, which is a SEAtrails community and could submit an application during the organization's upcoming call for projects. (The trail is not on USFS land, but the Forest Service could be a project partner by providing a letter of support and possibly in-kind support, such as GIS files and expertise.) Because of its role in disaster preparedness, it may also be worth exploring the potential for emergency preparedness funding.

Project Elements – This project consists of improvements to the existing Tsunami Trail in the City of Pelican. Improvements would extend approximately 0.5 miles, and would include grading to facilitate better drainage, with drainage structures as appropriate, and improvement to the surface treatment, such as gravel and wooden boardwalk. Some examination of site conditions would be necessary before deciding on a treatment, as gravel is less readily available locally but boardwalk may be unsuitable for some of the steeply graded segments. As the trail also serves as an evacuation route in the event of a tsunami, it may make sense to use two different materials: a harder surface treatment for the initial segment of the trail that leads from town to higher ground, thus facilitating the

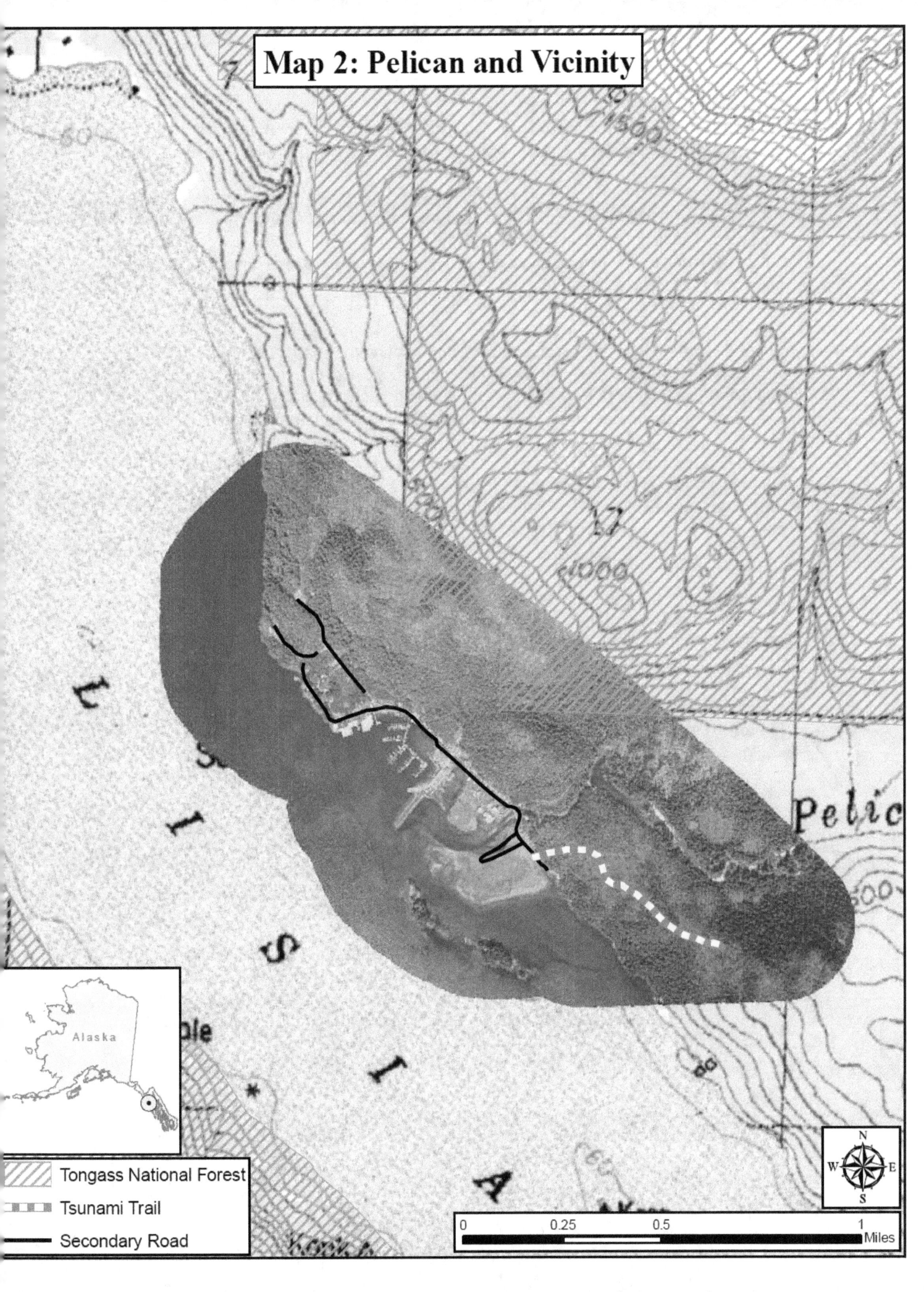

Map 2: Pelican and Vicinity

Pelic

Alaska

Tongass National Forest

Tsunami Trail

Secondary Road

0	0.25	0.5	1

Miles

N
W E
S

use of wheeled vehicles to transport the elderly, disabled and children in an evacuation; and a softer or more natural surface for the remainder of the trail, which is primarily recreational.

Development Feasibility Criteria - There has been no testing of engineering issues that would preclude its implementation. This project serves a critical need: saving lives of the local population by facilitating quick and efficient evacuation. Costs are not expected to be excessive. Usage is expected to be moderate for recreational purposes, and the project adds convenience and comfort, and lowers user costs, including energy expended.

Cost Elements – Widening of the trail from one- to three-person width implies a cross-section around 10 feet. At 0.5 mile segment length, the cost of grading the base layer and placement of either boardwalk or macadam or asphalt equals 26,400 sq. ft times the unit cost for material (including labor), which will vary according the material selected. Narrow bridges would be needed at several stream crossings, at an approximate cost of $3000 per linear foot of bridge. Field site investigation would determine the number of additional drainage structures (e.g., culverts and waterbars) beyond grading to achieve proper drainage. This cost is in addition to the surface treatment and bridge placement costs.

Chichagof Island: Freshwater Bay

Overview - Freshwater Bay (see Map 1 and Figure 2) is a popular area for picnics and family gatherings as well as wildlife viewing. It is also described by local stakeholders as an excellent candidate for the construction of boat haul-outs as well as expanded amenities such as picnic shelters and public restrooms. Usage of these amenities would probably be mostly local and therefore of limited economic impact; nonetheless, an improved site would be a valuable addition to the island's tourism infrastructure and could be used by eco-tour groups and independent travelers.

The provisions of SAFETEA-LU section 4407 related to Forest Service easements over state tidal lands offer a legal framework conductive to the construction of a marine access point at this location, if a public-private partnership could be arranged or external funding secured[15]. For example, via a suitable partnership with the State, boat docks and related infrastructure could be eligible for funding via the Federal Aid in Sport Fish Restoration (Dingell- Johnson) program or the Boating Infrastructure Grant program.

The State of Alaska has also recently announced that it plans to subdivide and offer for sale 150 acres of land at Freshwater Bay. Although this subdivision plan has not yet been made final, it offers the prospect of private land ownership and thus the ability for a partnership or concession arrangement with the private sector to provide recreation-related services.

---

[15] A broader discussion of the SAFETEA-LU provision and its relevance for the Tongass NF as a whole is included later in this section.

Project Elements – Components include new boat docks and related support infrastructure (e.g., lines to clean tanks, waterfront access boardwalk), and added public amenities such as covered shelters, picnic tables, and public restrooms. Commercial enterprises to support increased visitation (e.g., canoe and kayak rentals) may also be a development possibility, again dependent on the outcome of the proposed land sale and any restrictions that it may entail on commercial uses.

Figure 2: Freshwater Bay, Chichagof Island, Alaska

Development Feasibility Criteria – No testing has been conducted on possible engineering constraints, though the ability to provide restroom facilities would depend on the ability to provide water and sewer connections. No excessive costs are anticipated. Usage or demand is expected to be moderate, but it does serve several important transportation needs: it provides additional destination amenities at an established recreational site, it provides an intermodal connection via new dock facilities, it provides added convenience and comfort to eco-tour groups and to individual visitors, and it provides social benefits by connecting isolated populations to recreational and social activities. Additional transportation options and service may be required at Hoonah to provide access to Freshwater Bay for tourists without private vehicles (e.g., car rentals and/or jitney on-demand services).

Cost Elements – Recent USFS experience indicates that capital costs for a marine access ramp (boat launch) would be in the range of $100,000, or $150,000 or more for a full dock. A more detailed site plan and development program for the area would be needed to specify other costs in more detail, but the following considerations would affect the total cost:

- Square footage for required docks and waterfront boardwalk
- Total linear feet of utility lines by required hydraulic diameter
- Number of shelters and picnic tables
- Unit cost for a standard low-impact design shelter
- Number of public restrooms and unit costs
- Expected operations and maintenance costs

Analysis of Proposals – Wrangell Ranger District

The Wrangell Ranger District

The Wrangell Ranger District is located in the southern portion of the Tongass NF and comprises Wrangell, Etolin, and Zarembo Islands as well as numerous smaller islands and adjacent mainland areas. The road system on Wrangell Island includes approximately 100 miles of USFS roads that are open to motorized traffic, plus 35 miles of state and municipal roads. These routes are used extensively for multiple purposes, including timber and other industries, recreation, hunting, subsistence, and tourism. Most of the other areas within the Ranger District have much more limited road networks, though the northern portion of Etolin Island has about 70 miles of USFS roads that are used for recreation and subsistence[16].

The District's main population center is the City of Wrangell, with a population of about 2,300. Wrangell is served by the Alaska Marine Highway System and Inter-Island Ferry, as well as by twice-daily jet service and other air services. As with many communities in the area, Wrangell's economy has been built around timber, commercial fishing, cold storage, and related industries. Tourism also plays a significant role, with visitors arriving by cruise ship, ferry, and air. Cruise ship visitation has been higher in the past, but is currently limited to 1 to 2 calls per week during the season[17], primarily from smaller ships (50 to 225 passengers, compared to about 2000 passengers for the major lines).

Wrangell bills itself as the "Gateway to the Stikine River" and understandably much of the area's tourism is focused on the incredible recreation opportunities that the river offers. However, the city of Wrangell itself, along with nearby areas on Wrangell Island, possesses a number of high-quality visitor attractions that would benefit from expanded visitor access. A program of targeted investment in these opportunities would help to complement those of the Stikine River and to enhance Wrangell's reputation as a compelling tourist destination with a mix of year-round activities.

Wrangell has a lively downtown area and fascinating cultural and historical sites, such as Petroglyph Beach, Chief Shakes Island, and the Nolan Center and Museum. All of these are located within a mile or so of the ferry terminal, but the downtown area lacks the wayfinding signage and attractive pedestrian routes that would link these sites as a coherent whole. Some of these issues will be addressed by the City of Wrangell's upcoming downtown revitalization project, which will improve the aesthetics of Front Street via street and sidewalk improvements; create additional locations for visitor orientation and interpretive information; add sidewalk seating and shelters; and enhance the overall visual continuity of the area. The project is currently in the design stage, with construction expected later in 2008 or 2009.

---

[16] Wrangell ATM / EA, March 2007.
[17] The 2007 season was disrupted when the *Empress of the North*, the ship that visits Wrangell most frequently, ran aground near Juneau on May 14.

The Wrangell Cooperative Association also has plans to conduct renovation and repairs on Chief Shakes Island and to improve visitor information and access to this notable heritage site.

Wrangell Ranger District Concept

The confluence of the downtown Wrangell and Chief Shakes Island projects presents a valuable opportunity for the Forest Service to work with local partners to leverage these investments and enhance visitor opportunities in the city and in nearby areas of the Tongass NF. The Wrangell Ranger District concept is to leverage upcoming infrastructure projects and build partnerships to expand tourism on Wrangell Island. Based on discussions with stakeholders and analysis of potential funding sources and partnerships, the following specific projects would be pursued to support this broader concept:

1. Contribute to downtown wayfinding
2. Extend the Zimovia Highway bike trail
3. Build additional bike trails, with accompanying shelters along the routes
4. Create a system of group shelters with a reservation system
5. Develop a network of ski-in, ski-out cabins
6. Build a new cabin supporting snowmachine use
7. Formalize the portage trail on Etolin Island

As with Hoonah, the focus is on building on existing assets, opportunities, and projects. One proposal is directly tied to a revitalization project in Wrangell, and the others relate to expanding or formalizing existing trails and amenities and/or expanding the tourism infrastructure.

Contribute to downtown wayfinding
Overview - As noted above, the City of Wrangell is in the design stage for a downtown revitalization project that includes streetscape improvements, benches, shelters, and other elements to improve the pedestrian environment. It is designed to improve the aesthetic appeal of the downtown area for residents and visitors alike, while preserving the integrity of the area as a working waterfront. Although some new signage is already part of the plan, there is an opportunity for the Forest Service to support this effort through additional wayfinding elements. The emphasis would be on improving visitors' awareness of, and navigation to, recreational options along the roaded corridors of the Tongass NF adjacent to the City of Wrangell.

Project Elements - The town of Wrangell has completed a downtown revitalization master plan, designed to improve both functioning and aesthetics of the downtown, making it more attractive to tourists and enhancing economic development. This project proposes to design, integrate and implement a coordinated wayfinding system, compatible with local character and streetscapes, using a mixture of pedestrian-scale and vehicle-oriented signage. This signage would inform visitors of attractions, natural and cultural resources, and recreational opportunities on Wrangell Island, and would provide direction on how to use the USFS road system, in conjunction with the local street network within the town, to access these sites. USFS could also contribute in-kind technical expertise – e.g. in geology and silviculture – for sidewalk-level signage and interpretive panels.

Development Feasibility Criteria – There are no technical engineering issues that would block this project. Costs are reasonable, and the utility of the coordinated wayfinding system would be high. It provides a missing link in increasing the attractiveness of the island for tourism and recreational activity. It adds convenience and lowers the cost to the user of navigating the road system.

Cost Elements – Based on experience with similar projects, an architectural/engineering contract to design the system would be on the order of $30,000 to $50,000. Implementation of the system on the ground might be on the order of $50,000 to $75,000.

Extend the Zimovia Highway bike trail / build additional bike trails
Overview - These proposed projects are oriented toward expanding the range of local cycling trail options, which is both a recreational amenity in itself as well as a means of bringing more of the island within reach of Wrangell's visitors, especially walk-on ferry passengers and others without private vehicle access. Local stakeholders noted that Wrangell is starting to attract more birdwatchers and wildlife observers, and that additional bike trails and wilderness paths are an important part of drawing and supporting these visitors[18]. Expansion of the existing Zimovia Highway bike trail has also been listed as a priority by the Wrangell Chamber of Commerce. The construction of three-sided shelters along the routes would provide additional amenities for cyclists and protection from the weather during sudden squalls.

The existing asphalt-paved bicycle path starts just south of downtown and parallels Zimovia Highway for approximately 4½ miles, passing near the trailhead for Rainbow Falls and ending near Shoemaker Bay Loop Road (see Map 3). There are already many options for continuing bike rides on Forest roads, but many are rough and only suitable for mountain bikes. An extension of the paved path could offer a connection to recreation sites (including non-USFS areas such as Pat's Lake) and/or connect to the existing Nemo Loop Bike Route, which is a popular recreational loop with a mixture of crushed and uncrushed gravel sections. Since an extended bike route would likely cross through land under multiple jurisdictions (city, state, private, and USFS), stakeholder coordination and partnerships would be essential. Coordinated wayfinding signage would also help visitors navigate these areas in a seamless way.

Expansion of the Zimovia Highway trail could also be coordinated with a longstanding local effort to improve walkways and signage at the cemetery on Zimovia Highway near the Heritage Harbor. These improvements could be eligible for Transportation Enhancements program funding as "scenic beautification" and/or "historic preservation" along a Forest Highway route.

---

[18] Interview with Janelle Privett, Wrangell Chamber of Commerce.

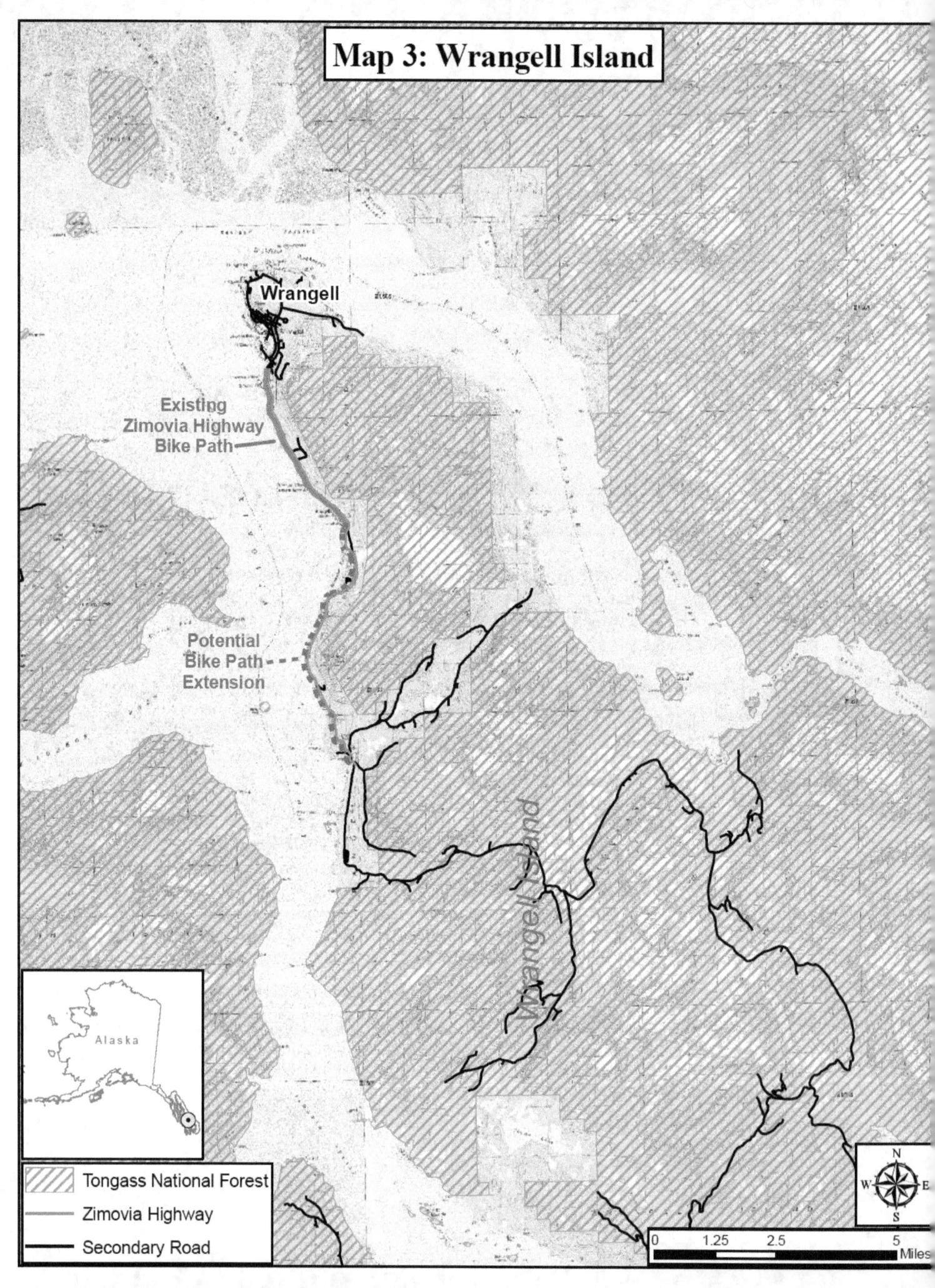

Map 3: Wrangell Island

Wrangell

Existing
Zimovia Highway
Bike Path

Potential
Bike Path
Extension

Wrangell Island

Alaska

Tongass National Forest

Zimovia Highway

Secondary Road

| 0 | 1.25 | 2.5 | 5 |

Miles

Additional bike path mileage and connectivity can have the effect of encouraging longer stays, for example as visitors plan on an additional night in town in order to bike an extra trail or visit another scenic or recreational site. It can also contribute to improved visitor satisfaction by providing access to a wider mix of activities beyond the historical center of Wrangell.

Project Elements – This project proposes extending an existing bicycle trail along the Zimovia Highway by several miles to connect with a separate but isolated loop road that could also be utilized by non-motorized ATVs or mountain bikes – the Nemo Loop Road. Bicycle-oriented wayfinding signage – for example, the mileage to the Nemo Loop Road– would also be a component of this project. Additional trails would also be added to the trailhead at Rainbow Falls, and to Pat's Lake, both desired visitor attractions. To the extent that space is available, three-sided shelters along the extended bike route would increase the desirability of the path by providing protection from the weather.

Development Feasibility Criteria – The existing bike trail lies between the road and the coastline. Although adequate right-of-way (ROW) appears to be available on the seaward side of the road along the length of the proposed route, assessment of engineering feasibility will require additional information on topography (as potential large cut/fill operations could be necessary to route the extension to the other side of the roadway. The project does serve several transportation needs: it provides additional access to visitor attractions; it does so in an environmentally benign way; it provides added convenience and comfort and lowers user costs.

Cost Elements – As mentioned above, technical engineering issues are uncertain enough to preclude a cost estimate at this time. Costs for asphalt-paved bike paths vary widely from project to project, though a lower figure (around $100,000 per mile) would likely be applicable in this case as there would be little to no land acquisition costs. The most important next step would be a site survey to determine whether (a) adequate ROW exists to simply extend the bicycle trail on the coastal roadside (and whether the soil could support a hard-surfaced trail); or (b) the trail would have to be extended on the land-side of the road. The site survey should also calculate rough estimates of cut and fill volumes and determine the net import of fill required.

Create a system of group shelters with a reservation system
Overview - This project addresses one of the identified gaps in Wrangell's tourism infrastructure: the relative lack of sheltered picnic and viewing areas for use by larger groups, such as those on local eco-tours. A reservation system to pre-book use of the shelters is also recommended as a way to manage these assets effectively and avoid conflicts between visitors and local residents intending to use the same sites. Though the direct economic impact of this investment would be limited in the short term, the shelters would enhance the quality of the visitor experience, which is an important factor in promoting repeat visits and in encouraging cruise-based visitors to return as independent travelers. Shelters that are suitable for group use could also be an asset in attracting convention and business groups to the Nolan Center, since the shelters could be used for organized excursions in the forest before or after the formal convention program.

Project Elements – This project proposes to site group shelters at strategic locations on the USFS road system in the vicinity of attractions such as prime wildlife viewing areas, scenic outlooks, picnicking areas and trailheads to hiking and bicycle trails on Wrangell Island. The shelters would be low impact design, compatible with the landscape, and sized to shelter groups of around 12 persons. A reservation system is also proposed to manage conflicting uses of these shelters and provide scheduling and certainty to group tour operators.

Development Feasibility Criteria – No studies have been conducted on technical engineering problems. Costs are not disproportionate to expected use and utility. Expected use is high. The project serves several transportation needs: it provides access to new visitor attractions and to hinterland areas not otherwise accessible; it adds greatly to comfort and convenience of the visitor; and it provides social benefits to isolated populations by enhancing access to recreational activities – including group activities.

Cost Elements – Costs would be based on the unit cost for a standard low-impact design shelter, and associated site preparation costs. In recent years, costs for the construction of remote cabins in the Tongass NF have been in the range of $114,000, and it is anticipated that shelter construction costs would be slightly lower due to the more limited functional requirements of a shelter and the ability to reach the construction site on the road system.

Develop a network of ski-in, ski-out cabins / build a new cabin supporting snowmachine use

Overview - These projects promote winter recreation, providing some seasonal balance to Wrangell's recreation and tourism profile and increasing the return on investments in tourism infrastructure. The ski and snowmachine trails are also a means of tapping into the Southeast regional and Alaskan travel markets, which are valuable complements to long-distance travelers. Ski-in cabins (or yurts) have become a popular winter recreation concept in several areas throughout the country, particularly Colorado. The commercial nature of the projects makes them best-suited to a public-private partnership or concession arrangement.

Project Elements – This project proposes a network of ski-in, ski-out cabins. The network of trails might also support snowmobile use. Wayfinding signage and mileage markers (mileage from trailhead, and mileage to cabin) would be a necessary component. Depending on the extent of the trail system and its relative proximity to the City of Wrangell, there may be some need for vehicular parking facilities at the trailheads, with the trailheads accessible via the USFS road system.

Development Feasibility Criteria – No studies have been conducted of potential engineering issues that would preclude development of the trail system and network of cabins. More detailed feasibility and siting studies would be required to identify locations with sufficient winter snow cover. Cost may be disproportionate to the expected use of the trail system and cabins. The project does serve a useful transportation and economic development need by providing access to new attractions and the backcountry. It also makes better use of the tourism infrastructure by providing off-peak season use, and tapping into the Southeast regional and Alaskan travel markets. It also opens up social and recreational opportunities to an isolated population. It provides intermodal connection (e.g., private vehicle to trailhead, then ski-in to cabin).

Cost Elements – As noted above, construction costs for USFS cabins are in the range of $114,000. The length and configuration of the trail network, the number of cabins, and potential vehicular parking facilities at the trailheads are the primary cost drivers. Specific information needed includes:

- Total square footage of the trail network (i.e., total length x cross-section)
- Number of cabins to be built
- Total square footage of vehicular parking lots at the trailheads
- Unit costs for a low-impact standard design cabin
- Unit costs for construction of vehicular parking lots (for choice of surface treatment, recommend permeable drainage surface treatment)

Formalize the portage trail on Etolin Island

Overview - This project refers to the informal portage trail on Etolin Island, a short overland connection (approximately 500 yards) between the waters of Anita Bay and Burnett Inlet. The portage is used extensively by Alaska Crossings, a Wrangell-based group that provides wilderness and educational programs for adolescents, on their canoe trips. In its current condition, the portage trail is a marshy bog, and passage is somewhat difficult. Alaska Crossings has suggested that it could work in partnership with USFS to harden the trail, for example by laying gravel, and to conduct periodic maintenance.

Formalization of the portage would create a valuable transportation link between two relatively sheltered bodies of water. It creates a "loop" around Etolin Island. This is important because of the value that recreational kayakers and canoeists place on being able to cover distances and see new places without exposing themselves to rougher waters. This connection would enhance the area's reputation among these boaters, who form an important market segment of recreational travelers. Perhaps even more importantly, this is a small project that is achievable in the short term, setting an early precedent for the formation of local partnerships and innovative maintenance arrangements.

Project Elements – This is a very simple project that formalizes an existing short (500-foot) portage trail over muddy soils on Etolin Island by providing adequate drainage and a hard surface treatment (probably boardwalk or well-drained gravel).

Development Feasibility Criteria – Although studies of this site have been informal, there are no known technical engineering problems that would preclude implementation. Costs would be marginal, usage is expected to be high, and users would experience added comfort and convenience, and lower 'user costs', at least in expended energy. The project provides a much needed intermodal connection.

Cost Elements – The major cost element is the labor and materials for covering the trail in gravel or other material. It is likely that much of the cost could be covered by partnerships with other organizations.

Figure 3: Anita Bay, Etolin Island, Alaska

Summary

Each project within the Wrangell scenario would have its own mix of potential funding sources and partnership arrangements. The bike trails, shelters, and cabins could be eligible for funding via the federal Recreation Trails Program, which provides funding for trails and trail-related facilities. The state of Alaska also has a Snowmobile Trails Program that would be an additional option for the proposed snowmachine trail. In each case, local matching funds (20 to 25 percent of project costs) would be required. While any discussion of partnership options should be considered preliminary, the City of Wrangell may be interested in pursuing one or more of these projects and providing matching funds as part of its economic development portfolio. Other local stakeholders including the Nolan Center and the Wrangell Convention and Visitors Bureau could also conceivably be brought into partnership. The local snowmobile club has expressed interest in partnering to build the snowmobile trail, and Alaska Crossings has offered to do almost all of the required work for the portage trail (requiring only regulatory approval and perhaps some in-kind support from USFS). Another potential partner is Watchable Wildlife, a national nonprofit group that promotes wildlife viewing opportunities.

Development feasibility analyses for projects in both the Hoonah and Wrangell Districts are summarized in Table 2, below.

le 2: Summary of development feasibility analysis by project

	Hoonah				Wrangell			
	Pelican: Tsunami Trail improvements	Freshwater Bay – MAP & improvements	Hoonah and Gustavus / Glacier Bay Ferry	Overland Route to Pt. Adolphus and/or Neka	Downtown Wayfinding System	Extension to Zimovia Hwy Bike Trail and add trails	Portage Trail on Etolin Island	G Sh
there geo-technical, hydrological or r engineering problems that make the osed project technically unfeasible?	No	No	No	Uncertain	No	Uncertain (topography requiring potential large cut/fill operations; inadequate ROW)	No	No
ost greatly disproportional to the length e project, or to its expected usage (or and)?	No	No	Uncertain	Yes	No	Uncertain	No	No
ether an improvement to an existing sportation facility, or a new project lity, are there data on existing usage , demand) or estimates of projected ge (or demand), both initial operational and design year?	No	No	No	No	No	No	No	No
qualitative sense, is usage or demand ected to be High, Medium, or Low?	Medium	Medium/High	Medium	Medium	High	High/Medium	High	Hi M
s the proposed project provide access connectivity to a new visitor attraction, a hinterland area not otherwise ssible?	No	Yes	Yes	Yes	Yes	Yes	No	Ye
s the proposed project provide an rmodal connection?	No	Yes	Yes	Yes	No	Yes (Bike/Pedestrian)	Yes	No
e proposed project critical for sistence needs?	Yes (Evacuation Route)	No	No	No	No	No	No	No
s the proposed project provide added venience, comfort, or lower user costs?	Yes	Yes	Yes	Yes	Yes	Yes	Yes	Ye
s the proposed project provide social usion benefits, i.e., providing access to al and economic activities for isolated ulations?	No	Yes	Yes	Yes	No	No	No	Ye
s the proposed project provide rnality benefits, i.e., lower energy sumption and/or air emissions and/or ding and/or soil and ground water amination?	Uncertain	No	No	No	No	Yes	No	No

Analysis of Proposals – Tongass-wide

Tongass-wide Concept: Traveler Information Systems

In discussions with local stakeholders, one of the most common themes was the need to provide independent travelers (and prospective travelers) with better information on local transportation options and conditions. Most visitors from the Lower 48 are accustomed to simply driving from one place to the next, so Southeast Alaska presents a logistical challenge in that most trips require arranging multiple trip segments by ferry, local air, or other means. Understanding ferry schedules and preparing a complete itinerary on one's own can be a complicated undertaking, particularly since airports and ferry terminals are not necessarily co-located, and multiple ferry services maintain their own schedules and sometimes operate from different docks within the same community.

Even where driving is possible, prospective visitors are unsure what to expect in terms of design standards, maintenance, and seasonal closures on Forest Service roads. They also seek information on practical matters such as mobile telephone coverage areas, amenities for RVs, and the availability of medical care and pharmacies.

Numerous stakeholders shared their perspectives on the need for improved travel-planning information. Sandy Marchbanks, mayor of Gustavus, said that she often takes telephone calls from would-be visitors who are confused about their travel options and local activities. Janelle Privett of the Wrangell Chamber of Commerce mentioned the need to provide RV-based and other independent travelers with detailed maps and information about road conditions. The SEAtrails organization also notes in its Trail and Transportation Master Plan, "Currently, visitors considering an independent recreation-oriented trip to Southeast must make a serious investment in time and research to plan their itinerary. Available information is largely piecemeal, or has to be obtained on a community by community basis." This creates the potential for unpleasant surprises, such as, "What do you mean I can't get out of Pelican until Friday without arranging for an expensive boat or plane charter?"[19]

With more and more Americans using the internet to plan their travel, there is a strong need for a "one-stop" online source for information about travel to, from, and within the Tongass NF and the Southeast region. One Tongass-wide concept is to promote independent travel to the Tongass through improved traveler information systems. One component of this would be a *"Milepost"-type guide with basic practical information* for each part of the area, along with information about USFS sites and amenities and other recreational and cultural opportunities. Detailed maps of local areas, showing appropriate transportation facilities and recreational options, would be available for browsing online and could be printed out for later use onsite. Another component would be an *itinerary planning service* that would allow prospective visitors to plan a complete trip through the Southeast region, highlighting the transportation options and intermodal

---

[19] *Trail and Transportation Master Plan*, prepared by Land Design North for Southeast Alaska Trail System (SEAtrails), May 2005.

connections required for each trip from "point A to point B."[20] For example, a visitor seeking to go from her home in Oregon to Hoonah would be presented with several options, such as flying to Juneau and connecting to an AMHS ferry; crucially, the itinerary would contain finer-grained information about links between the Juneau airport and the Auke Bay terminal, as well as a link to the ferry schedule and information about onward transportation options at Hoonah[21].

A number of travel planning websites for Alaska and the Southeast already exist, including sites sponsored by the Alaska Travel Industry Association and the Southeast Alaska Tourism Council. Though these sites offer maps and practical information (and in some cases even sample itineraries), they do not offer the point-to-point level of detail that travelers are seeking or that local stakeholders indicate would be worthwhile.

Evaluation

Due to its geography, Southeast Alaska necessarily has a wide range of "alternative" (i.e., non-automobile) means of transportation. Traveler information systems can be a useful means of promoting awareness and use of these options, while also helping to attract the independent travelers who contribute to the economic vitality of gateway communities. As noted earlier, independent travelers to Southeast Alaska also help to ensure the continued viability of the Alaska Marine Highway System. Based on a previous project to establish a travel planning site for National Park Service units, development costs for a website of this nature are estimated at $250,000. While not insubstantial, these costs are much less than the costs of conventional investments in roadway infrastructure or transit vehicles. Ongoing costs of website maintenance can also be shared through partnerships with tourism promotion agencies.

Given all of this, the project would be a good candidate for the Alternative Transportation in Parks and Public Lands program (and there is at least one precedent for such a project receiving funding through ATTPL). SEAtrails, local governments, convention and visitors bureaus, and Southeast Conference are all potential partners for developing the content of the online system. The Forest Service would supply information on USFS sites and could provide GIS and mapping data and the State tourism board could host the site.

---

[20] An example of this approach is the website for the National Park Service units in Massachusetts. NPS staff had noticed visitors' frustrations in trying to navigate Boston's confusing maze of one-way streets and the difficulties they faced in trying to gather information on over a dozen separate NPS units that are all within a half-day's drive. A travel-planning website now allows visitors to plan coordinated trips to one or more of the sites, based on geography or thematic interests. The site emphasizes public transportation options but also includes point-to-point driving directions and parking information. See http://home.nps.gov/applications/state/ma/

[21] Another example of this approach is the online "Smart Guide" for travel to Cape Cod, Martha's Vineyard and Nantucket. Point-to-point itineraries can be planned across travel modes. A traveler going from New York City to Martha's Vineyard would receive information about air routes, bus and ferry options, and connecting local public transportation once on the island. See http://www.smartguide.org/travelplanner2007.asp

Tongass-Wide Concept: Marine Access Point Study and Investment Strategy

Most locations in the Tongass NF are accessible only by water or air due to local geography, and waterborne transportation is thus what ties the Southeast region together. Marine access points (MAPs) are the mooring facilities that serve as the essential intermodal connections between the largely maritime transportation system and the various local road networks that provide access to uplands for recreational use, subsistence, and other economic activities. In the stakeholder consultation process for this study, one of the most consistent themes was the need for additional MAPs to support residents' local mobility needs as well as the growing recreation and tourism industries.

MAPs have typically been developed by private entities as part of timber harvests and mining. As these activities have diminished in recent years, MAP construction has waned and existing facilities have deteriorated. An additional barrier to greater investment in MAPs in the Tongass NF is the fact that legal title to much of the shoreline area over which the facilities would be built (i.e., submerged lands plus the inter-tidal area up to the mean high-water line) rests not with USFS, but with the State of Alaska. This creates a complex legal framework in which leases or easements would need to be individually negotiated for each potential MAP.

Section 4407 of the Safe, Accountable, Flexible, Efficient Transportation Equity Act: A Legacy for Users (SAFETEA-LU, Public Law 109-59), enacted in 2005, addressed this situation through a provision that establishes a reciprocal exchange of rights-of-way between the State of Alaska and the Forest Service. Under this exchange, the State would grant an easement to USFS for the construction of MAPs on State-owned tidelands adjacent to the National Forest. USFS, for its part, would grant easements to the State for the development and maintenance of transportation and utility corridors across USFS-owned lands, in accordance with the State Transportation Improvement Plan and other planning documents.

USFS and the State of Alaska have entered into a formal Memorandum of Understanding (MOU) to govern this exchange, which identifies 120 log transfer facilities and 230 MAPs within the Tongass NF. These sites have a variety of existing conditions: some have usable infrastructure, others have equipment in need of repair, and others have not yet been developed. At these sites, USFS may, to the extent consistent with resource preservation, construct, operate, and maintain docks, boat ramps, mooring buoys, floating breakwaters, and related facilities for public access without further specific authorization from the State.

These provisions open up numerous possibilities for improving visitors' access to recreation- and tourism-related sites across the Tongass, both at existing facilities and at undeveloped backcountry areas. Regional intermodal mobility would also be improved, as a network of MAPs would act as a "bridge" connecting otherwise-isolated road systems.

One specific example is the **Freshwater Bay** site in the Hoonah Ranger District (see pp.19-21), which emerged from this study as a recommended area for the construction of a MAP and is connected by road to the City of Hoonah. According to stakeholder input from the Wrangell Ranger District, another favorable area for MAP upgrades is at **Anan Creek**, an extremely popular wildlife observation area about 30 miles southeast of Wrangell. Access to Anan is via floatplane or boat, and the lack of a marine facility can make a vessel's approach and mooring precarious. It also means that visitors must climb over rocks along the beach as they transfer to the walking trail. Installing a marine facility at this site will improve the safety of mooring, open the Anan Creek wildlife observation experience to a wider range of visitors, and limit the impacts on the shoreline ecosystem.

Although many opportunities of this sort can be envisioned, no comprehensive strategy document has yet been developed for prioritizing investment in these MAPs and for maximizing their value. A full inventory and study of these sites is recommended as a means of developing this strategy.

Evaluation

A dedicated study of the sites identified in the MOU would allow for an analysis of their current condition and prospective contribution to mobility in the Tongass area and the local tourism economy, with the ultimate goal of generating a coherent strategy for prioritizing MAP investment. Specific tasks would include mapping their locations in relation to other transportation facilities, origin-destination travel patterns, and State planning corridors; conducting an inventory of existing facilities and their condition; identifying the type of MAP most appropriate for individual locations based on projected patterns of use; documenting ecological concerns and other issues; and synthesizing the information into a comprehensive investment strategy document. Costs are estimated at $200,000 based on information from USFS on the costs of similar studies.

Economic Benefits from Improving Southeast Alaska's Tourist Infrastructure

Introduction

This section of the report presents an estimate of the potential economic benefits to the Tongass National Forest's gateway communities that may result from the proposed improvements to the local transportation and tourism infrastructure. It is expected that these improvements will not only provide better transportation links within the Tongass region, but should also make Wrangell and Hoonah more appealing and attractive to visitors. In turn, this should encourage more tourism within these Districts of the Tongass National Forest, bringing economic benefits from a higher level of visitation.

Measuring the Economic Impact of the Proposed Improvements

In this study, a series of proposed improvements to the transportation infrastructure within Hoonah and Wrangell were examined. There are several proposed plans under consideration for each of these areas covering different levels of complexity, ranging from the initiation of a new ferry service to Hoonah to extending an existing bike trail. The transportation infrastructure improvements for the two areas in this study are:

Hoonah
- Overland route from Hoonah to Point Adolphus
- Improved access from Hoonah to the Neka Hot Springs
- New ferry service between Hoonah and Glacier Bay / Gustavus
- Pelican: Tsunami Trail
- Chichagof Island: Freshwater Bay

Wrangell
- Contribute to downtown wayfinding improvements
- Extend the Zimovia Highway bike trail
- Build additional bike trails, with accompanying shelters along the routes
- Create a system of group shelters with a reservation system
- Develop a network of ski-in, ski-out cabins
- Build a new cabin supporting snowmachine use
- Formalize the portage trail on Etolin Island

Tongass-Wide
- Traveler Information System
- Marine Access Point Study and Investment Strategy

For the economic impact analysis, how these transportation improvements affect visitation to the Tongass area, and subsequently economic activity, is of primary importance. For some of these improvements, the potential economic benefit will simply be too small to measure with any precision. A case in point would be the extension of the

Zimovia Highway bike trail in Wrangell, which, while certainly making the trail more useful and appealing, would likely only have a very marginal effect on attracting new visitors to the area. Decisions made to travel to Southeast Alaska, and to specific destinations within the region, would likely not hinge on the convenience of using this one particular bike trail, but rather on the attractiveness of the entire region as a tourist destination. In addition, measuring the effect on visitation numbers from this type of change would be extremely difficult and the utility of doing so would be very low. Even if the number of new visitors driven by this type of improvement could be quantified, it is likely to be so small, relative to the total number of travelers to the area, that it would not be possible to measure and isolate the economic impact. Other changes, however, such as the introduction of a new ferry service to Hoonah would be more likely to generate net new visitation and subsequently higher levels of activity.

Overall, of the proposed projects across both areas, the first three noted above for Hoonah have the highest potential for generating a noticeable affect in terms of increasing visitation to the area (through improved access). The other two for Hoonah would likely have a more limited economic impact.

For Wrangell, the development projects are more focused on improving the attractiveness of the area for tourists, rather than improving access to the area per se. As such, the near-term economic benefits of these changes may be limited in nature, but over time the appeal of Wrangell as a tourist destination should improve.

Given the differences in impact these improvements may have on visitation, and the difficulty in accurately measuring each of these effects, a collective approach to estimate the economic impact was undertaken. Through this approach, a series of potential total visitation gains, driven by the collective transportation improvements, was used as the basis for measuring the economic impact derived from this growth. Beyond this overall view, a more detailed look at the potential economic effects of the introduction of the ferry service between Hoonah and Glacier Bay was conducted. This proposed project lends itself to more fine-grained analysis due to the availability of visitation data from Glacier Bay National Park, though a number of assumptions still needed to be made regarding the frequency of the ferry service and ridership.

The vast majority of the area's tourism takes place during the May to September season. With two of the proposed transportation improvements in Wrangell specific to the *winter* season, however, a discussion on these changes is also included in the economic impact section. The potential economic benefits of an online trip-planning service are also examined.

Economic Analysis Modeling Overview

The analysis on the economic impact of tourism in the Tongass National Forest was done through the use of an economic impact model, Money Generation Model 2 (MGM2), developed for the National Park Service. This model is specifically designed to capture economic activity generated by tourists within local and regional communities in and around national parks. Since we are examining transportation improvement scenarios for the Tongass National Forest aimed at increasing the level of visitation and tourist activity, the model is well suited for the task at hand[22].The methodology behind this model, and other similar models, such as IMPLAN[23] or the Bureau of Labor Statistics' RIMSII, is well documented and is a commonly used method of measuring changes in a regional or local economy due to varying levels of consumer and business activity.

The first step in conducting this type of study was the creation of a baseline measure of the impact of tourism on the area under consideration. Using current visitation and spending totals, an estimate of the economic benefits stemming from the current level of tourism was modeled. Next, using the higher visitation level, as a result of the transportation infrastructure improvements, a second economic impact scenario was prepared. The economic activity due to these changes was then measured against the baseline, providing an estimate of the economic impact of making these improvements within the Tongass NF and gateway communities.

Economic Data

Input data for the economic analysis was sourced from the Alaska Office of Tourism Development. Through its Alaska Visitor Statistics Program V, tourism data for the 2006 summer season were obtained for Juneau, Hoonah and Wrangell. These data included the number of visitors arriving at each destination, the mode of arrival and the average spending per visitor across a number of categories, including lodging, souvenirs and food. This provides a level of detail that will allow for relatively comprehensive modeling of the visitation and spending profiles, and subsequent economic benefits, of tourism activity in Wrangell and Hoonah. Where possible we have strived to cross check and calibrate the information from the Alaska Office of Tourism Development through the use of data from other sources. In particular, we augmented the number of visitors arriving via cruise ship through data from the Cruise Line Agency of Alaska. Additionally, spending visitor spending totals from the Alaska Visitor Statistics Program V were compared with information from Juneau Visitor Bureau and the USDA Forest Service.

---

[22] The use of MGM2was detailed in the original statement of work.

[23] IMPLAN was developed in the 1970s by the USDA Forest Service and is now a product sold by Minnesota IMPLAN Group Inc

Measuring the Economic Impact of Tourism

Economic effects of tourist visitation to the Tongass National Forest will be measured by using the latest version of the National Park Service's Money Generation Model[24] (MGM2). This model, which was originally developed in mid-1990s, was built specifically to measure the economic effects of visitor spending on the local economies within and surrounding US national parks. Essentially this model views the economic benefits from visitor spending in a parks area as follows:

Economic Effects = Visitors * Average Spending per Visitor * Economic Multipliers.

While the average spending per visitor, multiplied by the number of visitors provides a measure of the direct economic impact tourism in the region, it is through the economic multiplier that we really gain insight into how visitor spending can benefit a local economy. Through economic impact modeling we have broken down the effects on a local economy into direct effects (as noted above) and secondary effects. The direct effects are quite straightforward; they capture and represent the income received by hotels, shops, restaurants etc. directly from visitors to the region. The secondary effects, which are classified as indirect and induced, arise as a result of this initial round of spending. In particular, indirect effects come from increased spending at supply firms (such as a local firm that supplies food to restaurants). Induced economic effects are a result of the higher level of economic activity that filters through the region due to visitor spending. Higher employment and income levels due to visitor spending will lead to further economic gains as workers in the local economy spend their money locally to the benefit of the economy. Combining the direct, indirect and induced effects of tourist spending in the region will provide a total economic impact from visitor spending within the region. The MGM2 model uses economic multipliers, which are applied to the direct spending to capture the total economic effects. Subsequently, the indirect and induced spending that filters through the local economy as a result of tourism activity can also be determined.

Using this methodology, the MGM2 model provides estimates of local sales, employment, personal income, and value-added that result from visitor spending. In the case of sales, the MGM2 model makes allowances for the fact that products sold locally are often not built locally. In particular, the model separates out the margin of sales that would accrue to a retailer, which would be less than the sales price (assuming that the good is produced elsewhere). The calculation is different for sales of services, where the portion of sales remaining in the local area is higher.

For employment, the MGM2 model determines the level of employment supported in the region by tourism activity. The employment measure generated by the model includes part-time and seasonal positions. The personal income measure includes wage and salary income, proprietors' income and employee benefits that arise due to visitor spending. Finally, value-added captures the contribution of the region being examined to the final

---

[24] The MGM2 Model; Daniel J. Stynes, Dennis B. Propst, Wen-Huei Chang and Ya Yen Sun, Department of Park, Recreation and Tourism Resources, Michigan State University

goods or services being sold. Essentially, value-added can be thought of as the final sales price of a good (service) after subtracting all of the non-labor production costs.

The MGM2 model is of particular use for our analysis of the Tongass NF as it incorporates multipliers that are keyed to activity around this type of region and allow us to specify the size of the area we are examining, from large metro area to rural area. These different types of regions would logically have different multipliers, reflecting different speeds at which visitor spending will disappear from the local economy due to the need to purchase goods and products from elsewhere to sell locally.

Using three key inputs, the MGM2 model allows us to identify and allocate economic effects to different types of visitors. For our analysis of the Tongass NF system, this is important as we will need to distinguish between visitors who arrive by cruise ship and visitors arriving by other transportation modes. In particular, cruise ship visitors typically spend only part of the day at a port destination, but stay on the ship overnight. Visitors arriving by ferry or air will have a different profile and are more likely to stay overnight in a local lodge, bed-and-breakfast, or campground. These differences will lead to different spending patterns that we capture and measure as part of our economic impact analysis. Within the MGM2 model we are able to isolate non-local day visitors (which would roughly match with a cruise visitor) and those visitors staying overnight in campgrounds or commercial lodging either inside or outside of the Forest boundaries. We are also able to apply various types of spending categories for each visitor. This allows the model to capture activity through different multipliers as they affect different sectors of the economy. As noted earlier, this is an important component of an economic impact study as it will allow us to distinguish between retail sales spending and spending on services, where leakages from the local economy are not as pronounced. Categories contained within the MGM2 model are presented in Table 3 below:

Table 3: Tourist Spending Categories

Motel, Hotel or B&B
Camping fees
Restaurants & Bars
Groceries & Take-Out Food/Drink
Gas & Oil
Other Vehicle Expense
Local Transportation
Admission & Fees
Clothing
Sporting Goods
Gambling
Souvenirs and Other Expenses

The granularity in the spending categories provided by the MGM2 model allows us to capture different types of spending between visitors and how that would affect the local economy. In particular, as mentioned earlier, these categories will allow us to distinguish between those visitors who arrive via cruise ship and only stay for a brief period of time and those who spend more time in the region and stay overnight.

Data and Model Input Assumptions

In this section, the data being used for our analysis are described along with its source. Further, any assumptions used to adjust or calibrate the mode input data are also described.

A critical element of any economic impact study is ensuring the accuracy and relevance of the input data being used. In particular, if possible it is advantageous in this type of study to use input data originating from a single source. This ensures that the timing and method of collection is consistent within the data and that these data should be comparable and consistent across the areas under review, allowing for meaningful comparisons. With this in mind, base data for this analysis were acquired from the Alaska Visitor Statistics Program V, published by the Alaska Office of Tourism Development. This is an ongoing statistical project undertaken by the State government and data from the summer 2006 visitor profile were used as the basis of this study. This study allowed us to capture both spending and visitation patterns and mode of arrival for Juneau, Wrangell and Hoonah/Icy Strait Point. To supplement these visitor totals, we used data from the Cruise Line Agencies of Alaska to measure the expected number of cruise visitors to each of these locations during the coming year. Spending totals were also compared with values published by the Juneau Visitors Bureau and the USDA Forest Service to check for relative consistency.

Table 4: Southeast Alaska Visitation

Number of visitors in 2006:	Total	As Share of Total Southeast Visitors	As Share Of Juneau Visitors
Juneau	1,034,000	89.1%	
Wrangell	34,000	2.9%	3.3%
Hoonah/Icy Straight Point	176,000	15.2%	17.0%
Source: Alaska Visitor Volume and Profile			

During 2006 there were more than 1 million visitors to Southeast Alaska. The majority of these (89.1%) went to Juneau, with Hoonah being the next largest destination (amongst those under consideration in this study) at 17%. Of more interest is how these visitors traveled to the region. As would be expected, the majority of tourists arriving in Southeast Alaska did so via a cruise ship. In Juneau, 70% of tourists arrived aboard a ship, while 63% of those visiting Hoonah/Icy Strait Point did so. Wrangell had a much lower number of cruise based visitors, at only 3% of total visitors to this destination arriving by ship.

Table 5: Visitor Transportation Mode

Entry Mode to Alaska (Percent of Total)	Air	Cruise	Highway/Ferry
Juneau	28%	70%	2%
Wrangell	67%	3%	29%
Hoonah/Icy Straight Point	36%	63%	1%
Source: Alaska Visitor Volume and Profile			

It is important to note that these figures represent the travel method by which visitors first arrived *within the state of Alaska*, not necessarily their method of arrival to each location. This artifact of the survey data is particularly relevant for Wrangell, as several cruises that call at Wrangell leave from Juneau; these visitors are thus counted as air arrivals even though their visitation and spending patterns in Wrangell would essentially be that of a cruise passenger. To adjust for this issue, we used data from the Cruise Line Agencies of Alaska as a reference point and calculated the total number of expected cruise visitors to each location based on scheduled berth capacity for the 2008 season. The table below summarizes these berth totals.

Table 6: Cruise Visitor Numbers

	Cruise Totals
Juneau	965,217
Wrangell	7,894
Hoonah/Icy Straight Point	110,146
Source: Cruise Line Agencies Of Alaska	

As a final calibration, the Alaska Visitor Volume and Profile data and cruise totals were adjusted based on information received from the USFS on the overnight lodging capacity at Hoonah and data on overnight camping visits within the Ranger District. The adjusted visitor data is presented in Table 7 below, showing the breakout between day visitors and overnight visitors.

Table 7: Total Visitor Numbers

Adjusted Visitor Data Based on 2008 Cruise Totals	Total	Day Visitor (Cruise)	Overnight Visitor (Air, Highway, Ferry)
Juneau	1,034,000	965,217	68,783
Wrangell	34,000	7,894	26,106
Hoonah/Icy Strait Point	176,000	166,000	10,000
Source: Alaska Visitor Volume and Profile, Cruise Line Agencies Of Alaska, Volpe Center Calculation			

The Alaska survey provides data on overall visitor spending habits. This information provides insight into the spending profile of visitors to each of the areas under consideration here. Of particular note is the large difference in spending patterns between visitors to Juneau and Wrangell as opposed to those going to Hoonah/Icy Strait Point. This is due in part to the greater share of Hoonah visitors coming via cruise ship and would suggest that the spending in this location is primarily on tours or outdoor activities, as indeed the data indicate.

Table 8: Visitor Spending Patterns

Average Expenditures in Southeast Alaska (2006)	Expenditure in Location	Lodging	Tours/ Activity/ Entertainment	Gifts/ Souvenirs/ Clothing	Food/ Drink	Rental cars/ Fuel/ Transport ation	Other
Juneau	$177	$9	$86	$66	$10	$3	$3
Wrangell	$115	$32	$15	$35	$17	$6	$10
Hoonah/Icy Straight Point	$53	NA	$31	$16	$5	NA	$1

Source: Alaska Visitor Volume and Profile

It should be noted these numbers are average spending across all visitors. This means that some of the figures need to be adjusted for correct interpretation when being entered into the economic impact model. In particular, the lodging category needs to be adjusted to reflect the actual spending by visitors on overnight accommodation, as opposed to spending by day visitors. The Juneau figure, for example, represents average lodging spending across *all* visitors to Juneau. With most of these arriving by cruise, the majority of visitors to Juneau will not require overnight accommodation other than their ship. As such, the total spending per visitor who stays overnight will obviously be higher than the reported (unadjusted) average of $9. We derive this new lodging average for visitors who stay overnight through a straightforward two-step calculation.

Equation 1: Total Lodging Spending = Average Lodging Spending * Number of Visitors

This first step calculates the total amount spent on lodging.

Equation 2: Adjusted Lodging Spending = Total Lodging Spending/Number of Visitors arriving via Air, Highway or Ferry

The second step then averages the total spending on lodging by those visitors who are likely to use it (i.e. non-cruise visitors).

The regional visitor spending profile after making these adjustments is detailed in Table 9. In the case of Hoonah, where there was insufficient survey data to have confidence in a lodging spending number, we assumed that an average value per visitor would be around $35. (This is the approximate cost for a USFS cabin, and also roughly half the cost of a double room in a local lodge in season.)

Table 9: Adjusted Visitor Spending Patterns

Region	Expenditure in Location	Lodging (non-cruise visitors)	Tours/ Activity/ Entertainment	Gifts/ Souvenirs/ Clothing	Food/ Drink	rental cars/ fuel/ transportation	Other
Juneau	$177	$135	$86	$66	$10	$3	$3
Wrangell	$115	$42	$15	$35	$17	$6	$10
Hoonah/Icy Straight Point	$53	$35	$31	$16	$5	NA	$1

Source: Alaska Visitor Volume and Profile, Volpe Center Calculation

Based on these data, the visitation and spending profiles for each of the three areas under consideration is as follows:

Table 10: Adjusted total Visitor Spending

Region	Total Visitors	Average Spending per Visitor
Juneau	1,034,000	$177
Wrangell	34,000	$115
Hoonah/Icy Straight Point	176,000	$53

Source: Alaska Visitor Volume and Profile, Volpe Center Calculation

Economic Impact Results

This section details the results of the economic impact model for the areas of Juneau, Wrangell and Hoonah (including Icy Strait Point). The first step in this analysis is the creation of a baseline measurement of the economic impact of visitors to each of the locations under consideration here. The baseline estimate represents the economic situation, *ceteris paribus*, from which we can measure the economic benefits of making changes in the local transportation system. The expected increase in visitation due to these improvements is added to the baseline visitation numbers and a new estimate of economic activity generated obtained through the MGM2 model[25]. Comparing these two results provides an estimate of the economic impact on the local economy. While our focus is on Wrangell and Hoonah, a baseline economic impact was also created for Juneau to serve as a Southeast regional comparison and benchmark.

Baseline Analysis

Juneau

Total Visitors:	1,034,000
Cruise Visitors (no overnight stay):	965,217
Non-Cruise Visitors (overnight stay):	68,783
Spending Per Cruise Visitor:	$168
Spending Per Non-Cruise Visitor:	$302

Baseline Economic Impact	
Direct Sales (Millions)	$219.03
Personal Income (Millions)	$83.34
Employment	4,550
Value Added (Millions)	$134.90

The MGM2 model estimates tourism in Juneau brings around $219 million in direct sales to the area. Before moving forward, it is useful to benchmark this model outcome to establish whether the calibration of the model is consistent with other estimates of this nature. In a recent study by the Institute of Social and Economic Research by the University of Alaska[26], the contribution of nature-based tourism to the Sitka, Juneau and Chichagof economies in 2006 was estimated at $250 million. The slightly lower estimate of $219 million in direct sales from the MGM2 model would appear to be consistent with the University of Alaska study, where Juneau does not constitute the entire area under consideration. Since our calculation was generated independently, the close correspondence in estimates of total sales gives us confidence in the model.

---

[25] The focus of this study is on spending by visitors to the region. Although cruise ship crews will spend money on shore in each location, with the level of cruise ship visits being held constant for each scenario this expenditure does not play a role in the analysis.

[26] The Regional Economy of Southeast Alaska, Steve Colt, Darcy Dugan, Ginny Fay, March 2007

Wrangell

Total Visitors:	34,000
Cruise Visitors (no overnight stay):	7,894
Non-Cruise Visitors (overnight stay):	26,106
Spending Per Cruise Visitor:	$83
Spending Per Non-Cruise Visitor:	$125

Baseline Economic Impact	
Direct Sales (Millions)	$4.26
Personal Income (Millions)	$1.55
Employment	100
Value Added (Millions)	$2.45

Hoonah/Icy Strait Point

Total Visitors:	176,000
Cruise Visitors (no overnight stay):	166,000
Non-Cruise Visitors (overnight stay):	10,000
Spending Per Cruise Visitor:	$52
Spending Per Non-Cruise Visitor:	$87

Baseline Economic Impact	
Direct Sales (Millions)	$10.81
Personal Income (Millions)	$3.90
Employment	253
Value Added (Millions)	$6.41

The baseline analysis clearly shows the importance of the cruise industry to Southeast Alaska's economy. This is particularly apparent when comparing the higher levels of economic activity derived from cruise related tourism at Juneau and Hoonah with Wrangell. Still, increasing the level of visits by non-cruise tourists is a desirable goal, particularly as these travelers tend to have a higher level of expenditure. Indeed, spending by non-cruise visitors is higher and inasmuch as it focuses more on services (e.g. hotels, tours), these monies will tend to have less leakage out of the local economy, compared with spending concentrated more on souvenirs or other retail purchases.

Additionally, growth in non-cruise visitors should also be easier for communities to handle, both logistically and in terms of social acceptability, particularly as these tourists may be more likely to arrive during off-peak times. By contrast, marked new growth in the high concentration of cruise visitors per docking could create additional peak-surge issues and overload the area's facilities. Further, there are likely to be resource-based limits to cruise tourist growth. Worth noting here is that the Huna Totem Corporation and the Hoonah community have generally expressed a desire to cap cruise dockings to one ship per day, which is consistent with their desire to employ local people. This clearly places a growth limit on the cruise industry, making gains in non-cruise based tourism more desirable. Non-cruise based tourism should also have a positive effect on the AMHS ferry system. These visitors will use this system more frequently (relative to cruise visitors), increasing demand during both on- and off-peak times. Higher usage levels should also help to shore up the finances of the ferry system and its sustainability as a transportation mode for the Southeast.

The infrastructure improvements being analyzed in this study would have a more pronounced affect on attracting non-cruise based visitors. As a result the second part of the economic impact analysis focuses on the benefits derived from these changes on the local economies of Hoonah and Wrangell.

Changes due to Transportation/Infrastructure Improvements

To gain an insight into how the economies of Wrangell and Hoonah will be affected by improvements in the transportation infrastructure, it is necessary to determine the increase in visitor volume due to these changes. By comparing the spending and income generated by this increased level of tourism, relative to the baseline numbers detailed above, we are able to determine the relative affect on economic activity.

Estimating the number of new visitors generated by the improvements in transportation infrastructure is therefore a critical component of this analysis. As noted elsewhere in this report, however, existing data (or estimates) on usage for the transportation features being proposed is not available. For example, in the case of the new ferry service between Hoonah and Gustavus/Glacier Bay there is still uncertainty as to the frequency and passenger capacity of this service, making it difficult to estimate how this new service may affect visitation numbers to Hoonah. In addition, as noted earlier, some of the other changes, such as improving existing bike paths, will likely have such a small effect as to make measurement of the change very difficult.

Given these data constraints, after some consideration, it was determined that examining changes in visitation as a percent of the current level would be a suitable way to approach this analysis. To do this, all of the transportation improvements under discussion in this report have been considered together in their effect on improving the attractiveness and appeal of Southeast Alaska to the non-cruise visitor. Using this approach, increases in visitation of between 1% and 3% were considered reasonable, based on professional judgment, for presenting a conservative analysis of the effects on local economic activity. Estimated changes in visitation for Wrangell and Hoonah are presented below in Table 11:

Table 11: Estimated Tourism Changes

Wrangell	
Total Visitors:	34,000
Cruise Visitors (no overnight stay):	7,894
Non-Cruise Visitors (overnight stay):	26,106
Estimated Increase Non-Cruise Visitors:	
1%	261
2%	522
3%	783
Hoonah/Icy Strait Point	
Total Visitors:	176,000
Cruise Visitors (no overnight stay):	166,000
Non-Cruise Visitors (overnight stay):	10,000
Estimated Increase Non-Cruise Visitors:	
1%	100
2%	200
3%	300

To provide some additional detail at a micro level, an exception to this top-down approach was made for the proposed ferry service between Hoonah and Gustavus / Glacier Bay. The introduction of this service creates a new transportation link in the area and would allow travelers visiting Gustavus/Glacier Bay to easily incorporate Hoonah into their itinerary. As a result, this improvement clearly has the potential to create new tourist demand within Hoonah. This analysis generates initial estimates of net impacts based on expected travel on this route, as estimated in the ferry analysis above.

Economic Impact Due to Higher Level of Non-Cruise Tourists

Wrangell

Increasing non-cruise based tourism in Wrangell could potentially boost direct sales in the area by between 1-2.5%, compared with the baseline. At the outer range of our analysis, a 3% increase in visitation would see sales increase to $4.37 million, compared with $4.26 million in the baseline scenario. The additional sales generated by the higher visitation would also have a positive effect on personal income, which would rise in a similar pattern to sales. These gains would come from adding between 261 and 783 new visitors to Wrangell per year as a result of the improvements in the transportation infrastructure.

Economic Impact		Increase in Wrangell's Non-Cruise Visitation		
	Baseline	1%	2%	3%
Direct Sales (Millions)	$4.26	$4.30	$4.34	$4.37
Change in Direct Sales (from baseline)		*$35,389*	*$71,611*	*$107,833*
% Change		*0.83%*	*1.68%*	*2.53%*
Personal Income (Millions)	$1.55	$1.57	$1.58	$1.59
Change In Personal Income		*$12,681*	*$25,661*	*$38,640*
% Change		*0.82%*	*1.65%*	*2.49%*
Employment	98	99	100	101
Change in Employment		*1*	*2*	*3*
% Change		*0.82%*	*1.66%*	*2.50%*
Value Added (Millions)	$2.45	$2.47	$2.49	$2.51
Change in Value Added		*$20,064*	*$40,601*	*$61,137*
% Change		*0.82%*	*1.66%*	*2.49%*

The total contribution to the region from this extra visitor activity, as measured by value added, would grow between 0.8%-2.5% based a 1-3% increase in visitation numbers. At a 1% increase in visitation, value added would grow by $20,064, while a 3% increase in tourism would add $61,137 to the local economy.

In comparison to Wrangell, Hoonah has higher levels of visitation but fewer overnight visitors. As a result, the projected economic gains from increases in independents visitors will not be quite as pronounced as in Wrangell. A 1-3% increase in non-cruise visitation will result in direct sales rising around 0.2% compared with the baseline.

Personal income and overall economic activity would increase at a similar percentage rate.

Hoonah

Economic Impact		Increase in Hoonah's Non-Cruise Visitation		
	Baseline	**1%**	**2%**	**3%**
Direct Sales (Millions)	$10.81	$10.82	$10.83	$10.84
Change in Direct Sales (from baseline)		*$10,666*	*$21,331*	*$31,997*
% Change (from baseline)		*0.1%*	*0.2%*	*0.3%*
Personal Income (Millions)	$3.897	$3.901	$3.904	$3.908
Change In Personal Income		*$3,586*	*$7,172*	*$10,759*
% Change		*0.09%*	*0.18%*	*0.28%*
Employment	253	254	254	254
Change in Employment		*1*	*1*	*1*
% Change		*	*	*
Value Added (Millions)	$6.406	$6.412	$6.418	$6.423
Change in Value Added		*5,862*	*11,724*	*17,587*
% Change		*0.09%*	*0.18%*	*0.27%*

* One full-time equivalent or less

Employment[27] in both areas is expected to grow marginally at best due to the estimated increases in visitation levels. This economic model output appears reasonable given the relatively conservative set of assumptions about visitation growth. It would be likely that increases in activity of this magnitude, spread out across a four- to five-month season, would not require a large addition to the workforce.

Measuring the Effect of a Glacier Bay/Gustavus-Hoonah Ferry Service

For the purposes of modeling economic impacts , it is assumed that ferry passengers would be day-trippers to Hoonah and that their level of spending would be consistent with that other day visitors (primarily cruise visitors) to Hoonah, as detailed above.

---

[27] Within the MGM2 model, reported jobs include part-time and seasonal positions and are not a full-time equivalent.

Estimates of the Hoonah-bound ridership for this proposed ferry service (see ferry analysis above) also need to be adjusted to avoid possible double-counting of visitors who would visit Hoonah by other means even in the absence of the ferry service. Thus, the analysis takes a very conservative estimate of net new visitation, at 526 person-days per season. These levels imply positive, albeit relatively small, effects on economic activity in Hoonah: an estimated $32,756 increase in direct sales and a subsequent $19,562 increase in value added.

Economic Impact	Increase in activity due to Ferry Service	
	Baseline	With Ferry-BasedVisitors
Direct Sales (Millions)	**$10.81**	**$10.844**
Change in Direct Sales (from baseline)		*$32,756*
% Change (from baseline)		*0.30%*
Personal Income (Millions)	**$3.897**	**$3.909**
Change In Personal Income		*$11,895*
% Change		*0.31%*
Employment	**253**	**254**
Change in Employment		*1*
% Change		*0.31%*
Value Added (Millions)	**$6.406**	**$6.425**
Change in Value Added		*$19,562*
% Change		*0.31%*

The changes in economic activity are marginal enough to have little to no effect on total employment, though personal income would be bolstered by around $6,000 to $12,000 due to the additional economic activity driven by a new ferry service. This is largely consistent with findings from the literature review on the effects of tourism on traditional economies (see Bibliography, p. 82), in which it is noted that the effects can be more pronounced in income terms than in employment terms. Note, however, that these results consider only near-term, direct visitor spending in Hoonah. Over the longer term, Hoonah could benefit more broadly by becoming a base of accommodation for independent visitors seeking to spend some time at Glacier Bay.

Winter Season Visits

The network of ski-in and ski-out cabins proposed for Wrangell could potentially play a role in enhancing this area's attractiveness during the winter season. Growth during this period would certainly be beneficial, particularly as it may help to balance out changes in the level of economic activity between the peak summer tourist season and the rest of the year. The relatively small nature of the Wrangell winter market, however, does not allow for good data upon which to base a formal analysis. A review of the Alaska Visitor Volume and Profile Study for Fall/Winter 2006/07 noted that only 1% of all visitors to Alaska during this period went to Wrangell, with less than 1% of these visitors staying overnight. Indeed, the study was unable to quantify the number of visitors to Wrangell who were there for vacation/pleasure and stayed overnight. In addition, no spending data for Wrangell amongst fall/winter visitors were available.

Still, there are some data points on winter tourism from this study that are worth noting. Taking a broad view of the Southeast region, the length of stay for all fall/winter overnight visitors was 10.1 nights. This compares with an average stay of 5.7 nights for summer visitors[28]. Although the fall/winter figure does contain overnight stays with family/relatives, it suggests that visitors during the winter season do have a propensity to spend more time in the area. In addition, the winter season appears to generate a higher level of spending per person. According to the Alaska Visitor Volume and Profile Study for Fall/Winter 2006, visitors to Juneau spent an average $414, while summer visitors spent an average $177. The difference between these figures is in large part is due to a higher level of demand for lodging during the non-cruise season. These data suggest that increasing winter visitation would have a positive economic effect on the Tongass National Forest. Nonetheless, further study on this topic would be needed to provide the level of detail and data required for a formal impact analysis.

Tongass NF / Southeast Alaska Traveler Information System

A trip-planning and visitor assistance website would help to ensure that the improvements to the transportation infrastructure being discussed here, and the enhanced appeal they will give the Tongass region, are communicated to potential visitors. Given the current lack of a truly comprehensive online resource for planning trips to this region, this initiative would serve the tourism business in the region particularly well. Indeed, research presented through the Alaska Visitor Statistics Program indicates that the internet is a vital source of information for tourists to the Southeast. In particular, according to the summer 2006 Study, 66% of visitors to the Southeast and Juneau used the internet as a resource for trip planning. For Hoonah and Wrangell the percent of visitors using the internet as a planning tool was 96% and 71% respectively, with smaller numbers actually booking their trip online as well. During the winter season, an estimated 64% of visitors to Juneau used the internet for trip planning, with around 54% booking their trips online. These data show clearly that tourists planning to visit Southeast Alaska and the Tongass National Forest view the internet as an important component of trip research and planning. As such, improving the online presence of the Tongass National Forest and its amenities and attractions for visitors would be a valuable

---

[28] This includes cruise ship passengers. Those arriving by air spent an average 6.2 nights, while those arriving by highway/ferry spent 5.3 nights

tool in growing the region's tourism economy. Although its impacts cannot be estimated quantitatively in the absence of fine-grained data on tourist decision-making, the traveler information system would certainly be expected to have a positive impact on the local visitor economy, via two distinct pathways: first, by reducing the informational barriers to visitation, the system would help bolster the number of lucrative independent visitors; and second, by helping visitors to plan a seamless trip and avoid unpleasant surprises such as missed ferry connections, the system would improve visitor satisfaction and encourage repeat visits.

Summary and Next Steps

This report summarizes the outcomes from a transportation system opportunity study for the Hoonah and Wrangell Ranger Districts of the Tongass National Forest. The study's focus is the identification of opportunities for using the existing assets of the USFS transportation system to generate recreation- and tourism-related economic development opportunities. Initial identification of project proposals was based on a stakeholder-driven process in which residents of these communities, particularly those engaged in the recreation and tourism industries, offered their opinions on the most promising opportunities. The goal of involving stakeholders was not only to draw on local knowledge and expertise, but also to lay the groundwork for continuing stakeholder involvement and the fostering of partnership arrangements.

Stakeholders' ideas for transportation-related projects were analyzed along several dimensions, including expected benefits and economic impacts; degree of local support; scope, cost, and complexity; and funding and partnership options. While very few of the identified opportunities were based exclusively on existing transportation facilities, the resulting set of recommended project proposals does reflect the study's focus on leveraging existing assets. The recommendations include:

- **Measures to improve the access and efficiency of the existing transportation network**, including Wrangell wayfinding signage and a Tongass-wide online trip planning website
- **Improvements or expansions of current transportation assets to improve connectivity and recreational options,** including upgrades to the Tsunami Trail, extension of bike trails on Wrangell Island, and formalization of a portage trail on Etolin Island
- **Targeted investments in tourism infrastructure** to support recreational use along the road and maritime transportation networks, including a marine access point and visitor facilities at Freshwater Bay, group shelters on Wrangell Island, facilities to support winter recreation on Wrangell Island, and a study of potential marine access points using reciprocal right-of-way exchanges
- **New and/or improved intermodal access to existing recreational resources**, with a focus on tying together isolated road systems and providing additional recreation and tourism opportunities. Specific concepts include new access to Neka Hot Springs, a land route to Point Adolphus, and new ferry service between Hoonah and Glacier Bay / Gustavus.

These projects were then analyzed in greater depth to identify implementation options and constraints, as well as expected economic impacts. The transportation analysis provides a basic assessment of viability and cost elements and highlights the steps needed to move from opportunities to implementation. (It is important to note that this analysis is an initial review and is prior to the required processes of the National Environmental Policy Act; the transportation scenarios represent opportunities and options rather than formal NEPA alternatives.)

The economic analysis is based on a well-established model of visitor spending in gateway communities, and indicates that these projects could produce significant increases in local sales and income, though the impact on overall employment would be relatively minor. In addition to the calculated changes in direct visitor spending and economic impact, these investments would also set the stage for future growth in the visitor economy in these communities.

This study is intended not merely as an analytical exercise, but as the first step in the process of implementing these transportation projects and realizing their benefits. The table below summarizes some of the major next steps along the path to implementation.

Project / Concept	Partnership and Funding Options [29]	Other Next Steps
Multimodal access from Hoonah to Neka Hot Springs and Point Adolphus	ATPPL; Recreation Trails Program; concession agreement	Site surveys
Ferry service between Hoonah and Glacier Bay / Gustavus	Partnership with Huna Totem Corporation, NPS, and/or City of Gustavus; concession agreement	Further vessel and route analysis, visitor survey to support ridership projections
Tsunami Trail upgrade	SEAtrails (priority project) via City of Pelican	Engineering site survey
Freshwater Bay MAP and visitor amenities	Boating Infrastructure Grants or Dingell-Johnson via State; Recreation Trails	Engineering site survey
Wrangell wayfinding	City of Wrangell; Transportation Enhancements	Development of plan for signage content, placement, and design vocabulary
Wrangell Island bike trail extensions	ATPPL; Recreation Trails Program; Transportation Enhancements; City of Wrangell; SEAtrails; Watchable Wildlife	Engineering site survey
Group shelters	Recreation Trails; Wrangell CVB and outfitters	Consultation process on potential locations and partnerships
Winter recreation (ski-in, ski-out cabins and snowmachine trail)	Recreation Trails; state Snowmobile Trails program; SEAtrails	Consultation process on potential locations and partnerships
Formalize portage trail on Etolin Island	Alaska Crossings	Environmental review and USFS approval
Online traveler information system	ATPPL; state and regional tourism agencies	Consultation on partnership options and development of website requirements
Marine access point study and investment strategy	SEAtrails via municipalities; ATPPL	Scoping work, inventory

[29] References to specific funding sources or partnerships are not meant to imply that eligibility has been determined, or that USFS has committed to a partnership or funding application.

Beyond these specific projects, the stakeholder process in this study also indicated that there are opportunities related to pursuing new partnerships with local groups to maintain and improve transportation facilities. The most prominent example is the possibility of entering into maintenance agreements with Alaska Native groups via the Indian Reservation Roads program. Smaller-scale arrangements could also be put in place to formalize some of the operations and maintenance activities that are already taking place, for example in Hoonah where outfitters and guides clear snow and keep trails open on an *ad hoc* basis.

Appendix A – Tongass National Forest Transportation System Opportunity Study Draft Memorandum on Foundational Research, November 30, 2006

Tongass National Forest (Tongass NF) is situated in southeast Alaska, an area blessed with many natural and cultural resources that is undergoing significant economic change. Many of the region's communities are suffering from economic distress related to the decline of timber and other resource extraction industries. The Volpe National Transportation Systems Center is supporting the United States Department of Agriculture Forest Service (USFS) in their efforts to examine how the existing assets of the Tongass NF can be better used to generate local economic development opportunities. In particular, the Forest Service road network, originally designed for timber extraction, is an asset that could be adapted for use in facilitating new tourism- and recreation-oriented development.

This memo summarizes the first component of this effort, which has focused on foundational and context-setting research It is designed to shed light on the pertinent issues and trends that will shape the course of future work and analysis. At this early stage of the project, the memo does not formulate specific economic development proposals or identify site-specific transportation needs; these will be the outcomes of subsequent activities built around stakeholder consultation.

Part I of this memo presents a socioeconomic profile of the region, with summary-level overviews of relevant issues such as demographics, industries, employment, transportation and tourism. Part II comprises a summary of research on issues related to the transition from a resource economy to a more diversified economy with contributions from tourism and recreation. It includes a mixture of general "lessons learned" and specific case studies.

I. Socioeconomic Profile of Southeast Alaska

This section provides a brief overview of the sociological and economic conditions prevailing in southeast Alaska. The goal is to ensure that subsequent phases of this project proceed from an appropriate understanding of the area and its people. The Volpe Center did not perform any primary data-collection for this section, but instead compiled information from multiple sources, including the 2000 U.S. census and Forest Service reports. As Hoonah and Wrangell (and their environs) are the principal initial focus of this study, more detailed information on these locations is presented wherever available.

Demographics
Approximately 73,000 people live in southeastern Alaska, spread out across approximately 29,000 square miles of islands and mainland. Tongass NF covers about 80 percent of this area, and much of the rest is held by other federal and state agencies, or by Alaska Native corporations. As a result, population densities within settled areas are much higher than the raw population and area figures might suggest[30].

---

[30] Southeast Alaska Comprehensive Economic Development Strategy. Prepared for the US Department of Commerce by the Southeast Conference and Central Council Tlingit and Haida Indian Tribes of Alaska, April 2001.

The chart below provides a basic demographic profile of the region and some of the smaller geographic areas within it, based on data from the most recent decennial census in 2000. In some cases, more recent information is available from the 2005 American Community Survey and is presented in the narrative sections below.

	United States	Southeast Alaska	Skagway-Hoonah-Angoon Census Area	City of Hoonah	Wrangell-Petersburg Census Area	City of Wrangell
Total Population	281,421,906	73,082	3,436	860	6,684	2,308
Median Age (Years)	35.3	35.9	37.8	35.6	37.2	39.1
Female	50.9%	48.6%	46.2%	47.0%	48.0%	48.5%
White	75.1%	71.2%	58.1%	28.7%	73.0%	73.5%
American Indian or Alaska Native	0.9%	17.1%	35.0%	60.6%	16.1%	15.5%
Median household income	$41,994	n.a.	$40,879	$39,028	$46,434	$43,250
Persons below poverty level	12.4%	7.6%	12.8%	16.6%	7.9%	9.0%
High school graduate or higher	80.4%	90.1%	84.4%	80.5%	85.8%	82.2%
Bachelor's degree or higher	24.4%	27.3%	21.6%	15.4%	16.3%	13.7%
Homeownership rate (Owner-Occupied Housing Units)	66.2%	63.7%	62.9%	77.7%	70.4%	67.9%

Source: US Bureau of the Census, 2000, summary file 3. The "southeast Alaska" column comes from Kline, J., L.E. Kruger, and R. Mazza. "Demographic trends in southeast Alaska." In Mazza, R. and L.E. Kruger, tech. eds., *Social conditions and trends in southeast Alaska*. Gen. Tech. Rep. PNW-GTR-653.

Taken as a whole, the region's population possesses levels of income and education that are near or above the national average. Regional averages, however, tend to obscure the significant disparities between communities, particularly those outside Juneau. Comparisons with national figures also present a methodological challenge due to the region's cost-of-living, which includes higher prices for many consumer goods but also much greater opportunities for subsistence use of fish and game[31].

One thing that is clear from the statistics is that over the past 15 years, southeast Alaska's demographics have followed a much different course from that of the United States as a whole. During the 1990s, for example, per capita incomes rose 12 percent nationally and most parts of the country enjoyed fairly robust economic growth. Southeast Alaska was instead experiencing a much more mixed picture, with some areas experiencing economic decline during the 1990s. Average incomes in the region fell by about 2 percent during this decade. The city of Hoonah was particularly affected, with annual per capita incomes falling from $19,386 in 1989 to $16,097 in 1999 in inflation-adjusted terms (a 17 percent decline). As incomes decreased, the share of households living below the poverty line increased.[32]

For the region as a whole, population growth in the 1990s was much more modest than the national average, and many communities saw a net loss of population. The limited data that have been collected since the 2000 decennial census suggests that some of these trends have continued. During the five-year period between 2000 and 2005, the populations of the Wrangell-Petersburg and Skagway-Hoonah-Angoon census areas declined by an estimated 6.6 and 9.0 percent, respectively[33].

Industry and Employment
Discussions of population growth and income are intimately linked with changes in the region's industrial base and sources of employment. For many decades, the economy of the region has been based primarily on a mixture of resource extraction industries – timber, mining, and fishing – and related manufacturing and processing. Public administration has also been an important component, due in part to the presence of the Forest Service and the many state offices in the capital city of Juneau.

Timber production has dropped substantially since 1990 due to a number of factors, including changes in market conditions, revisions to public land management policies, and unfavorable movements in foreign currency exchange rates. During the period from 1990 to 2000, the annual timber harvest from Tongass National Forest fell from 470 million board feet (mmbf) to 120 mmbf[34].

---

[31] Kline, J., L.E. Kruger, and R. Mazza. "Demographic trends in southeast Alaska." In Mazza, R. and L.E. Kruger, tech. eds., *Social conditions and trends in southeast Alaska*. Gen. Tech. Rep. PNW-GTR-653. Portland, Oregon: USDA Forest Service, Pacific Northwest Research Station, 2005.

[32] Ibid.

[33] US Bureau of the Census, American Community Survey, 2005.

[34] Southeast Alaska Comprehensive Economic Development Strategy. Prepared for the US Department of Commerce by the Southeast Conference and Central Council Tlingit and Haida Indian Tribes of Alaska, April 2001.

The Southeast Alaska Comprehensive Economic Development Strategy documents the decline of the timber industry and the wide-ranging negative repercussions that this has had for the region: increased unemployment, adverse impacts on related industries, and reduced revenues for local governments. Other industries related to natural resources have held slightly more steady, but face challenges of their own. For example, the fishing industry is dealing with declining market share for wild Alaskan salmon, the effects of competition from farmed salmon produced in other regions, and the need to regulate local fish stocks[35].

U.S Census data from 1990 and 2000 reveal some of the shifts in employment in the region. The charts below represent employment levels by industry for the Census areas that cover the two communities of interest, Hoonah and Wrangell.

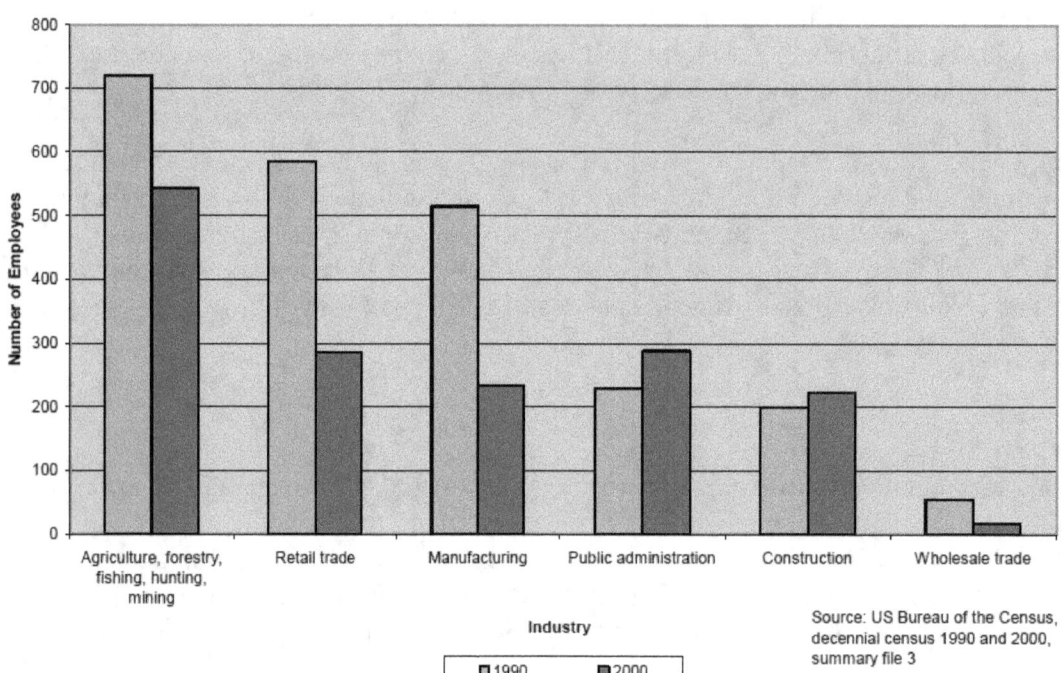

Wrangell-Petersburg Census Area, Employment by Industry, 1990-2000

Source: US Bureau of the Census, decennial census 1990 and 2000, summary file 3

---

[35] Ibid.

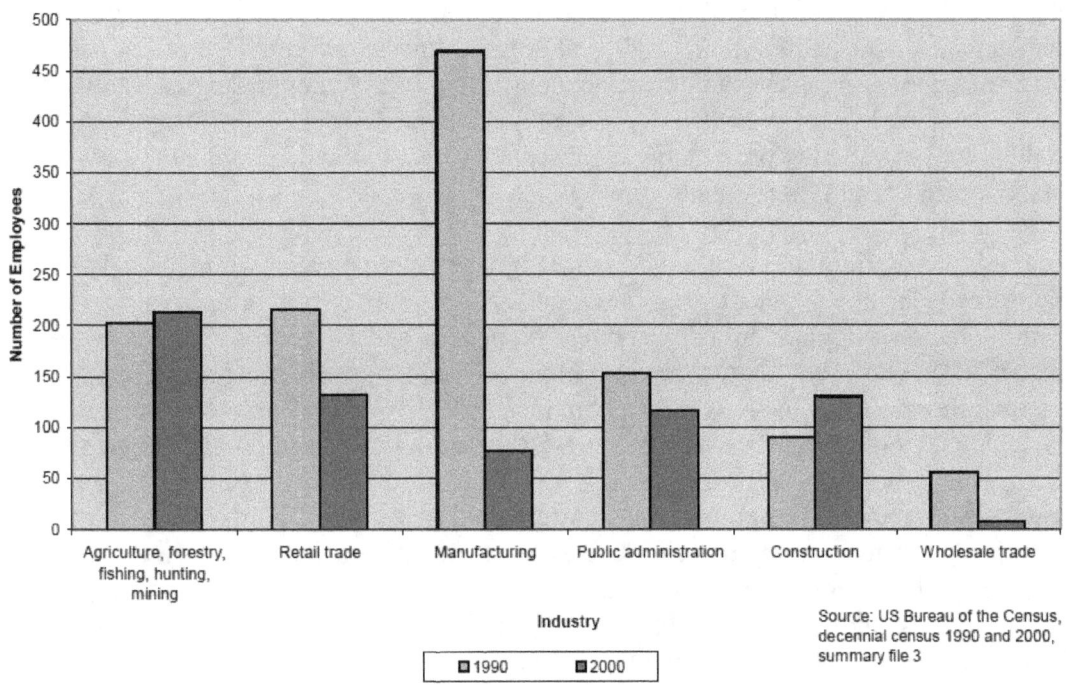

Skagway-Hoonah-Angoon Census Area, Employment by Industry, 1990-2000

Source: US Bureau of the Census, decennial census 1990 and 2000, summary file 3

One of the few bright spots in the local economic picture has been tourism. Visitors have been coming to this part of Alaska in small numbers since the late Victorian era, but the scale of the industry and its associated economic impacts grew substantially in the 1980s, after a round of cruise ship expansions and growth in the Alaska cruise market[36].

Tourism-related economic growth is difficult to track because of the lack of a specific Census category for such employment, which cuts across categories such as retail trade, transportation, entertainment, and accommodation, and includes many part-time and seasonal positions. (Another complicating factor is that the decennial Census is conducted in April, prior to the start of the main tourist season, and therefore may not capture the full extent of such employment.) Tourism also has many indirect effects on other industries by increasing the effective market size and creating demand for ancillary goods and services. As a rough estimate, however, the economic impact of tourism on the southeast Alaska region has been estimated at about $80 million per year, supporting about 4,100 jobs;[37] growth in this sector of the economy has been noted in numerous reports and studies. Additional detail on tourism in the region is presented in the Tourism section below.

---

[36] Cerveny, Lee K., Tourism and Its Effects on Southeast Alaska Communities and Resources: Case Studies from Haines, Craig, and Hoonah, Alaska. USDA Forest Service, Pacific Northwest Research Station, PNW-RP-566, July 2005.

[37] McDowell Group, Inc., *Economic Impacts of Alaska's Visitor Industry*, May 1998, cited in G. Fay et al., *An Economic Vision For a Prosperous Alaska*, Prosperous Future Development Coalition, February 2004.

Language and Culture

The region has a fairly high degree of linguistic diversity. In Hoonah, for example, nearly one in six residents uses a language other than English at home. However, knowledge of English is nearly universal; in most areas the share of residents without proficiency in English (defined by the Census as speaking English less than "very well") is 2 percent or less. Therefore, language issues would not be expected to present any significant barriers to the development of tourism or recreational opportunities in these areas.

On the contrary, the continuing use of indigenous languages – principally Tlingit and Haida – could be an asset in the development of cultural and heritage tourism programs. Approximately 1 percent of the region's population, i.e. just over 700 people, speaks Tlingit or Haida as their first language[38]. These mother-tongue speakers are mostly older people, raising concerns about the languages' prospects over the longer term, but there are also local efforts to preserve the languages, and many other people have some interest or second-language proficiency in them.

An extensive discussion of this region's rich culture would be well beyond the scope of this memo, but it is clear that one thing that residents of southeast Alaska have in common is the high value they place on being connected to the area's natural resources. As one assessment puts it, "Personal use of forest and marine resources is considered by many to be a vital component of local culture, lifestyle, and family provisioning."[39] Many people in the region also share concerns about how natural resources are being managed and, more broadly, what the long-term picture of the region looks like.

Transportation

The region's transportation patterns are very different from those in much of the rest of the United States, as many communities are on islands or are otherwise accessible only by ferry or airplane. While most towns have small internal road networks, the only connections to the continental road system are at Haines, Skagway, and Hyder. Inter- and intra-regional transport of freight, vehicles, and passengers takes place using a mixture of the Alaska Marine Highway System, private ferry services, and an air network that comprises 12 airports and 33 public seaplane floats. The Forest Service also maintains about 3,600 miles of forest roads within Tongass NF, about a third of which are suitable for use by ordinary passenger vehicles[40]. The map on the next page, taken from the region's 2004 transportation plan, shows the existing transportation network.

---

[38] Gordon, Raymond G., Jr. (ed.), 2005. Ethnologue: Languages of the World, Fifteenth edition. Dallas, Tex.: SIL International. Online version: http://www.ethnologue.com/, accessed November 2006.

[39] Allen, S.D., G. Robertson, J. Schaefers. *Economies in Transition: an assessment of trends relevant to management of the Tongass National Forest.* Gen. Tech. Rep. PNW-GTR-417. Portland, Ore.: USDA Forest Service, 1998.

[40] State of Alaska, Department of Transportation and Public Facilities, *Southeast Alaska Transportation Plan*, August 2004.

Concepts for developing tourism and recreational opportunities must take account of these transportation patterns and constraints, as well as any new projects that could affect local and visitor traffic, such as the proposal to extend a road to Juneau.

Tourism in Southeast Alaska

According to several analyses that have been conducted, three main attributes attract visitors to the region: the scenic beauty of its waterways, glaciers, and forests; the opportunities for outdoor recreation; and the unique cultural attractions, particularly those related to the cultures of Alaska Natives[41]. The growth of tourism to southeastern Alaska is due largely, though not exclusively, to the development of a popular Alaska cruise ship product, which offers access to these elements in a convenient "package," typically as part of a voyage through the Inside Passage.

As the number of voyages and the size of the vessels on these routes have increased over the years, so too has the number of visitors. While exact figures for the region as a whole are not available, visitation statistics for Juneau are often used as a rough proxy measure, since almost all ships visit Juneau along their way. The chart below documents the growth in cruise ship passengers visiting Juneau. As the chart shows, during the period from 1990 to 2005, the number of cruise-based visitors to Juneau rose from approximately 237,000 to over 949,000, the equivalent of over 9 percent annual average growth.

Cruise Ship Visitors to Juneau

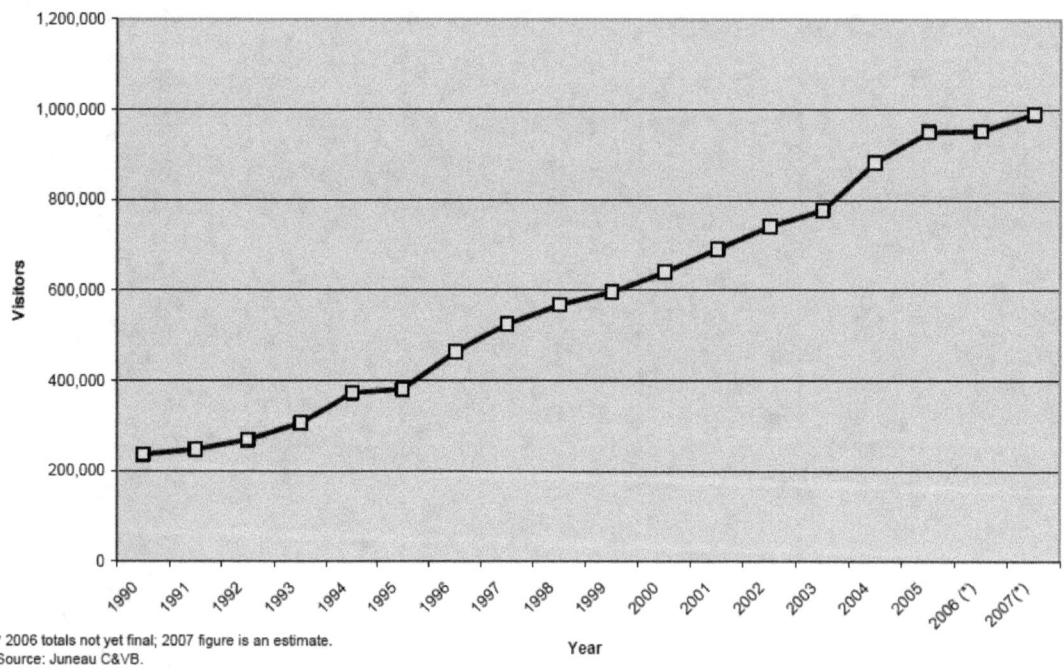

* 2006 totals not yet final; 2007 figure is an estimate.
Source: Juneau C&VB.

---

[41] See, e.g., City and Borough of Juneau, *Juneau Tourism Management Plan*, 2002.

According to the Juneau Convention and Visitors Bureau, in recent years the rapid pace of tourism growth has begun to level off, due in part to capacity constraints with Juneau's port infrastructure. For 2006, the C&VB projected a 1 percent increase over 2005 levels, and for 2007 is projecting an increase of about 4 percent over 2006 levels. This would bring annual cruise-based visitation to nearly 1 million in 2007.

Tourism and related industries were estimated in 1998 to contribute about $80 million to the region's economy[42], and the figure is likely to be significantly higher now, given that visitation levels have risen substantially. One more recent estimate from the University of Alaska's Institute of Social and Economic Research puts the figure at around $250 million per year[43]. This includes visitor spending at the relatively new Icy Strait Point area just outside of Hoonah, a growing destination for cruise ships that was developed by the Huna Totem Corporation and is staffed primarily by Tlingit people[44].

Despite this picture of economic growth and local involvement, the experiences of specific communities in the region have varied. This is particularly true in cases where cruise lines have made abrupt decisions to change their port-of-call schedule or eliminate a stop altogether. (In the next phase of the project, discussions with stakeholders will explore the cruise lines' decision-making process in this area.)

The region also receives a substantial number of "independent" visitors who arrive by air and/or make use of the Alaska Marine Highway System. Different data sources list independent travelers as constituting between 15 and 25 percent of the visitor total. There are some indications that the number of independent travelers to the region has declined over the past 10 years, though traffic at the Juneau airport has experienced relatively steady growth[45]. In general, less is known about the non-cruise visitor market and there is less "hard data" on visitor counts[46].

Rising levels of visitation have created friction in some southeast Alaska communities over issues such as noise from flight-seeing tours over residential neighborhoods and downtown traffic congestion during the summer season[47]. In more rural areas, charter fishing and hunting are sometimes seen as a threat to commercial operations and to traditional subsistence hunting and fishing. More frequent interactions with strangers have also changed the dynamics of more remote towns and led to debates within Alaska Native communities about the proper approach to tourism[48]. More broadly, there is a concern about a loss of local control, in that decisions made

[42] McDowell Group, Inc., *Economic Impacts of Alaska's Visitor Industry*, May 1998, cited in G. Fay et al., *An Economic Vision For a Prosperous Alaska*, Prosperous Future Development Coalition, February 2004.

[43] Dugan, Darcy. "The Economic Contribution of Southeast Alaska's Nature Based Tourism," Institute of Social and Economic Research, University of Alaska, 2006.

[44] Icy Strait Point, Press Release, March 1, 2005.

[45] Cerveny, Lee K., *Tourism and Its Effects on Southeast Alaska Communities and Resources: Case Studies from Haines, Craig, and Hoonah, Alaska.* USDA Forest Service, Pacific Northwest Research Station, PNW-RP-566, July 2005.

Juneau Economic Development Council, Juneau Economic Overview, July 2006.

[46] City and Borough of Juneau, *Juneau Tourism Management Plan*, 2002.

[47] Collaboration Juneau, Inc., Stakeholder Meeting Minutes (various dates 2004-2005).

[48] Cerveny, Lee K., *Tourism and Its Effects on Southeast Alaska Communities and Resources: Case Studies from Haines, Craig, and Hoonah, Alaska.* USDA Forest Service, Pacific Northwest Research Station, PNW-RP-566, July 2005.

by large cruise lines and other corporations have large local ripple effects. There is a perception that local entrepreneurs and tour operators are being replaced by international firms with few ties to the community[49].

Market trends
Several trends at work in the worldwide tourism industry have implications for the southeastern Alaska market. These include[50]:

- Greater emphasis among visitors on being environmentally responsible in their travels, and having more of a "learning/education" experience;
- Rising interest in cultural activities, and the links between tourism and cultural development and resource protection;
- Growth in eco-tourism, adventure travel, and "soft-adventure" tourism; and
- Increasing interest in thematic tourism (i.e. tour packages centered on a particular personal interest such as Civil War history, Shakespeare, textiles, etc.).

Due to the continuing importance of cruise-based visitors for the region, trends in the North American cruise industry as a whole are also particularly relevant. Notable trends include a movement toward shorter cruises and smaller ships, as well as growing interest in "group cruising" related to weddings, reunions, and other social functions[51]. Another industry-wide trend is the increasing "vertical integration" of cruises, with the cruise line itself owning and operating the shore excursions. This has the effect of reducing opportunities for local businesses to serve these visitors;[52] it is therefore a factor in evaluating economic development prospects.

Cruises to Alaska continue to be dominated by four companies which together control over 90 percent of the market: Princess, Holland America, Royal Caribbean / Celebrity, and Norwegian. The most common product is a 6-8 day cruise departing from Vancouver, though there are now many other variations, and cruises take place during a season that runs from May to September. Alaska cruises have enjoyed a high level of customer satisfaction[53].

Visitor demographics
This section provides a brief profile of visitors to Alaska and, where available, more detailed information about cruise- and non-cruise based visitors to the southeast region in particular. (The definition of "visitor" varies from one data-gathering agency to another; most of the differences revolve around the difficulty of separating local and regional travel from long-distance travel.)

Looking at the state as a whole, visitors to Alaska come primarily from the United States (86 percent), particularly the west coast; Washington, California, and Oregon are the most common

---

[49] Collaboration Juneau, Inc., Stakeholder Meeting Minutes (various dates 2004-2005).
[50] City and Borough of Juneau, *Juneau Tourism Management Plan*, 2002.
[51] Ibid.
[52] G. Fay et al., *An Economic Vision For a Prosperous Alaska*, Prosperous Future Development Coalition, February 2004.
[53] City and Borough of Juneau, *Juneau Tourism Management Plan*, 2002.

states of origin. Another 9 percent of visitors are from Canada, and 4 percent come from other foreign countries[54]. While summer is by far the busiest season, with 84 percent of visitors coming during the May to September period, winter visitation has been growing at a slightly faster rate overall. Winter visitors contain proportionately more business and convention travelers.[55]

About half of trips to Alaska by out-of-state visitors are leisure-related, another quarter are business-related, and the remainder consist of visits to friends and relatives or trips for other purposes. Most visitors to the state are between the ages of 25 and 64 and have household incomes over $50,000.[56]

The southeast region of Alaska differs from the rest of the state in that most of its long-distance visitors arrive by cruise ship, making the demographics of the cruise market particularly relevant to this project. Cruise-based visitors to Juneau (again, a proxy for the regional cruise market) average 55 years of age, with average household incomes of $95,000. Fifty-three percent are college graduates.[57] This makes this group somewhat older, wealthier, and better-educated than the general population, as summarized in the table below:

	Average Age	Mean Household Income	Bachelors Degree or Higher
US average (2000-2004 Census data)	35	$60,628	24%
Cruise visitors to Juneau (2001)	55	$95,000	53%

An intercept survey of a sample of cruise visitors to Juneau in 2005 showed that 83 percent were from the U.S., 8 percent from Canada, 3 percent from the United Kingdom, and 6 percent from other countries – fairly similar to the statewide average. Most cruise visitors came in groups of two, with relatively few single travelers (6 percent) and an overall average group size of 3.2 persons. Cruise-based visitors to Juneau spent an average of $100 per person on tours and shore excursions in Juneau and another $86 on other items while in town[58].

A survey of a small sample of <u>non</u>-cruise visitors to Juneau showed non-cruise visitors to have a roughly similar demographic profile, with an average age of 46 years and an average household income of $80,000. Median party size was 2.0 persons. Non-cruise visitors reported an average trip duration of 7 days total in the area, of which an average of 3 days were spent in Juneau. By contrast, the typical Alaska cruise lasts 6-8 days and spends one day in Juneau. Among non-

---

[54] US Department of Transportation, Bureau of Transportation Statistics, American Travel Survey, 1995.

[55] G. Fay et al., *An Economic Vision For a Prosperous Alaska*, Prosperous Future Development Coalition, February 2004.

[56] US Department of Transportation, Bureau of Transportation Statistics, American Travel Survey, 1995.

[57] Survey on Juneau Visitor Center Needs, prepared for the City and Bureau of Juneau by the McDowell Group, November 2001.

[58] Juneau Cruise Visitor profile, 2005, prepared by the McDowell Group for the City and Borough of Juneau, December 2005.

cruise visitors, average daily spending was $291 per party, including $97 for lodging, $51 for food, and $39 for entertainment and sightseeing.[59]

Overall, the pattern that emerges from this data is that of an older, affluent visitor base, albeit one that is diversifying as cruise lines make inroads among younger travelers. Having traveled over 800 miles – and in many cases, much farther – to reach southeast Alaska, most visitors appear inclined to stay longer and/or spend more on local tours and entertainment than visitors to other areas. Just as an example, the average leisure visitor to Boston, Massachusetts, stays for 2.2 days and spends just $41 per day exclusive of lodging.[60]

---

[59] City and Borough of Juneau, *Juneau Tourism Management Plan*, 2002.
[60] Boston Convention and Visitors Bureau, 2005 visitor statistics.

II. What Factors Contribute to a Successful Transition to a More Tourism- and Recreation-Based Regional Economy? Findings from a Literature Review

There is now a considerable body of academic literature on tourism's role in local and regional economic development, some of which specifically addresses the more specific questions about the transition from a natural resources-based economy and the role of transportation in that transition. However, as one author in this field notes, "There is little, in the literature, which addresses economic restructuring specifically in the context of tourism in regions which are peripheral in both economic and geographical terms, particularly islands."[61] Therefore, some of the research findings on this topic relate to areas that are dissimilar to southeast Alaska in terms of their location, proximity to major population centers, and accessibility by road. However, an effort has been made to concentrate on findings from areas that share some of southeast Alaska's geographic and social characteristics.

Fundamental Principles

This section identifies some of the high-level "lessons learned" on local tourism development, based on the experiences of places around North America and, in some cases, overseas. It has been condensed and synthesized from a large number of articles from the academic literature, government reports, and the press. A full list of citations for the articles reviewed can be found in the appendix, though footnotes are used here for direct quotations or specific concepts.

Begin with realistic expectations about the potential impacts of tourism.
Tourism undoubtedly can serve as an engine for local employment. Tourists need food and lodging; they hire local people as naturalists and tour guides; they buy local arts and crafts; and they provide many other job opportunities through the variety of goods and services they consume. Beyond the immediate income that this brings, tourism-related jobs can help to stem the tide of out-migration and stabilize the community.

However, many authors stress the fact that tourism should not be viewed as a panacea for a community's economic ailments, nor can it serve, in most cases, as a one-to-one replacement for jobs that have been lost in other industries. Examples abound of local tourism development efforts that have not lived up to expectations. Even among the success stories, the unfortunate fact remains that tourism-related jobs are often part-time and seasonal, with lower wages than those in the natural resource industries and few, if any, fringe benefits such as employer-paid health insurance. Seasonality is a particular concern in Alaska where more than four-fifths of all tourists come during the May-to-September season.

Authors in this field therefore suggest that tourism should be regarded not as the sole avenue to economic recovery, but rather as *one element* of a diversified local economy. Just as portfolio diversification allows investors to achieve greater returns with less risk, a diversified local economy provides protection against changing market conditions. Tourism-related diversification can bring opportunities for extra income even if it does not create significant

---

[61] Baum, T. "The decline of the traditional North Atlantic fisheries and tourism's response: the cases of Iceland and Newfoundland," *Current Issues in Tourism*, Vol. 2, No. 1, pp. 47-67, 1999.

numbers of new jobs. There is also some specific evidence that diversified economies – e.g. with both timber production and tourism employment – fare better in the long run than areas that concentrate on just one industry[62].

Communities should plan for tourism as part of a comprehensive community planning process, not in isolation.

If there is one overarching theme in the literature, it is that the development of local tourism opportunities must not happen in isolation, but as part of a broader planning process that reflects the community's values. Local residents must make well-considered decisions about how to balance the benefits of tourism with the costs in terms of impacts on local resources and values. The following issues are typically at the forefront:

- Natural resources: Human activity inevitably impacts natural resources, and economic growth leads to increased consumption and additional waste. Improved public services such as electricity, water, and sewerage can invade, consume, and pollute natural resources. Tourists themselves impact the natural environment by hiking, camping, fishing, and hunting in the wilderness. Communities that consider promoting tourism must decide how to use their natural resources and wilderness. There is often a conflict between consumptive tourist activities such as hunting and fishing, observational tourist activities such as bird watching, and other recreational activities such as boating and hiking. These activities might also affect residents' traditional resource usage by, for example, encroaching on traditional hunting and fishing grounds. Communities must make collaborative decisions about how resources are to be used and how much of their local environment they are willing to share with visitors.

- Cultural heritage: Many indigenous peoples (including Native Alaskans) have successfully maintained important aspects of their culture. Tourists are attracted to these communities in part to experience their unique way of life. This can help preserve local culture by providing economic incentives for maintaining local arts and crafts, and religious and other traditional activities. Preserving the local culture, therefore, is important to the cultural and economic climate of the area. In addition, by educating tourists about native culture, locals can encourage respect and support for their traditions among "outsiders." However, an influx of tourists can also have a negative effect on culture. Tourist infrastructure such as hotels and restaurants change the physical characteristics of towns and villages. In addition, tourists bring their own culture with them, and accommodating tourists requires some cultural shifts. For example, restaurants must serve food that appeals to tourists – food that might not be consistent with local eating habits.

- Economic opportunity: Even from a strictly economic point of view, tourism imposes costs as well as benefits. Visitors use local infrastructure and generally expect to rely on municipal services such as police and fire protection, roads, and bridges. Communities need to ensure that there is a mechanism for recouping the cost of these services, for

---

[62] Wilson, S., and D.R. Fesenmaier, "Factors for success in rural tourism development," *Journal of Travel Research*, Vol. 40, November 2001, 132-138.

example through a port charge or accommodation tax. More broadly, communities need to devise a plan for ensuring that local people can actually benefit from tourism – that jobs are open to them and that tourism-related businesses give preference to local suppliers for their goods and services. In the absence of pro-active planning, it is not uncommon for multinational, vertically integrated companies to dominate the tourism market and to make minimal use of local labor, products, and services.

In short, *integrated tourism*, as some authors term it, ensures not only that "tourism is integrated into broader economic and social development contexts, goals and decisions" but also that tourism is structured in a way that ensures that local people control the decision-making process and can benefit from the jobs and income generated.[63]

Successful tourism development requires both leadership and partnership.
The economic development literature often notes the value of having a respected community leader who can serve as a "champion" for local economic development, both tourism-related and otherwise. Champions help develop a community-wide vision of the future, are willing to take risks or suffer economic losses to achieve this vision, and use their influence and persistence to keep projects moving forward despite delays and setbacks.

At the same time, important decisions must be made with substantive community input, not just by a small elite. Tourism development programs are strengthened by partnerships, both public-public (i.e. among different government agencies or across different levels of government) and public-private. Several authors also stress the importance of strong cooperative relationships between local governments and their business communities, noting the strongly complementary nature of public sector investments (such as upgrades to roads and water systems) and private sector investments in hotels, restaurants, and tourist facilities. Neither set of investments is sufficient on its own.

Maintain and enhance the quality of the "product."
Consumers have an ever-growing number of options for travel and tourism, and competition for tourist dollars is fierce. To be successful in attracting visitors year after year, communities must burnish their reputation for providing good value for money. Some of the factors cited in the literature include the amenities available to visitors and the courtesy and professionalism of the people that visitors encounter.

Communities must also work hard to protect the resources that attracted visitors in the first place, even as the community grows and changes in response to tourism. While hotels, supermarkets, parking garages, and the like all provide convenience for visitors, they can – if not planned carefully – destroy the historical feel, "authenticity," or ambiance that visitors are seeking. This is particularly true for cultural and heritage tourism, but applies to recreational areas as well, especially those that offer the prospect of unspoiled wilderness or unique experiences. In the era

---

[63] Oliver, T., and T. Jenkins. "Sustaining Rural Landscapes: the role of integrated tourism," Landscape Research, Vol. 28, No. 3, July 2003, 293-307.

of the internet, news of an area that has been "spoiled by overdevelopment" or has "lost its charm" travels very quickly.

Local Tourism Development in Alaska: The Five A's
The Alaska Division of Community and Economic Development (DCED) highlights five factors as essential to the development of a successful local tourism industry: attitude, access, accommodations, attractions, and advertising[64]. This provides a useful framework for analyzing the more specific factors that influence the growth of tourism in Alaska's local communities.

Attitude refers to the simple fact that visitors like to feel welcome, and that tourism is most successful when local residents interact with tourists in a warm and hospitable way. Attention must also be paid to the particular needs of visitors when considering such things as the opening and closing times of shops and services. This is one of the most intangible factors related to tourism but can be very important to the long-term viability of a tourism destination.

Access: The ability of visitors to reach an area is a necessary pre-condition for any sort of tourism development. Economic models of the tourism market posit a strong inverse relationship between visitor demand and the cost of access (where "cost" includes not only pecuniary costs but also time and inconvenience.) In most of North America, rural tourism is heavily dependent on highway access to major population centers, and some authors (though they constitute a minority) go so far as to say that successful tourism development is just not possible for areas that are beyond a reasonable driving distance of an urban area. This reality is a particular concern for tourism in Alaska, especially for southeast Alaska, most of which is only accessible by ferry or airplane and is not connected to the continental road system.

As the experience of the past few decades has shown, however, limited transportation options do not necessarily foreclose the possibility of a successful tourism industry. There are several reasons for this. First, tourists who travel in rural Alaska are self-selected for their willingness to take lengthy trips. Second, there is growing evidence that the *reliability* of the transportation service and the *predictability* of travel times are among the most important determinants of the travel decision – in many cases, more important than the speed or duration of the travel. As an example, the DCED cites the willingness of visitors to travel to the Pribilof Islands in the Bering Sea, despite the cost and distance, because of the reliability of the flights. Third, there is also evidence that the very inaccessibility or "separateness" of an area can become part of its appeal, especially for islands for which a true water crossing is needed; this often produces feelings in visitors of "difference" from their urban lifestyle and greater opportunities for relaxation or for exposure to different cultures and folkways[65].

Accommodations: Any area that wants to attract tourists must be able to accommodate them – that is, to provide them lodging, food, public services, local transportation, and shopping (at least for essentials). In considering the most appropriate types of accommodations, communities must

---

[64] State of Alaska Division of Community and Economic Development. Undated. *Alaska Community Tourism Handbook: How to Develop Tourism in Your Community.*

[65] Baum, T. "The decline of the traditional North Atlantic fisheries and tourism's response: the cases of Iceland and Newfoundland," *Current Issues in Tourism*, Vol. 2, No. 1, pp. 47-67, 1999.

understand the types of tourists they want to attract and the needs and preferences of those travelers. Accommodations should also be commensurate in size and services offered with the scale and type of tourism being offered. Independent travelers looking for a wilderness experience require entirely different tourist infrastructure than travelers who arrive for a day trip from a cruise ship; birdwatchers may differ from sportsmen in their demographic profiles, party size, and expectations about lodging.

Accommodations must be tourist-friendly: they must have convenient hours, be safe and clean, and have conscientious staff. Matching the supply of accommodations with their demand is a delicate task. Communities must be able to meet peak demand but also be able to sustain the accommodations during the off-season.

Attractions: The presence of impressive natural resources and native culture by itself is not sufficient for developing a robust tourism industry. Tourist destinations must create an identity and develop attractions that take advantage of that identity. This requires local people to make decisions about what type of travelers they want to attract and how best to leverage local resources to deliver the tourist experience travelers want.

In rural Alaska, attractions are usually centered around natural resources and cultural heritage. However, villages cannot be all things to all people. Villages that want to become a port of call for cruise ships, for example, must develop an identity as an accessible destination that can be comfortably experienced in a few hours. In contrast, areas that want to attract birdwatchers or hunters must develop attractions such as guided tours and hunting lodges.

Advertising: In most cases, merely building tourist facilities will not make tourists come. Travelers have to know about the area, learn what it has to offer, know how to get there, and know what to expect when they get there. This requires marketing. The State of Alaska, local Chambers of Commerce, and various community development and tourism organizations offer marketing assistance and opportunities. However, each community must also develop marketing strategies and materials that specifically highlight what it has to offer. The goal is to differentiate the community from others that offer similar tourist experiences.

This marketing must be carefully targeted towards the types of tourists the community wants to attract. Marketing can be geared toward agencies that provide tour packages and cruises, or directly at tourists who are looking to travel independently. Modern marketing techniques allow "micro-targeting" of particular markets of interest, such as birdwatchers or deep-sea fishermen. It is also not uncommon for communities to develop marketing strategies pitched specifically at certain overseas markets to which they may have a particular link or affinity; for example, some regions in Pennsylvania highlight their German heritage via advertisements that run in German-language media outlets in Europe.

Case Studies of Transition

Many communities in the United States and across the globe have faced the challenge of making the transition from an economy based largely on natural resources to one with a stronger contribution from tourism and recreation. This section presents some "case studies" of communities that have addressed this transition in different ways, with an emphasis on places that share some characteristics with the Tongass area, such as geographic remoteness, inaccessibility by road, strong seasonality, and low-density settlement.

Copper River Delta – Cordova Shorebird Festival

The Copper River Delta in south-central Alaska shares a number of characteristics with southeast Alaska. Most notably, it is an area of outstanding natural beauty, in this case a vast wetland that supports a wide variety of plant and animal species. It is also accessible only by ferry and air service, and its population is largely clustered in small settlements. The economy of Cordova, the delta's gateway town, is dominated by a natural resource industry – commercial fishing – but has begun to diversify into tourism in response to downturns in that industry.

One of the key factors in the development of a tourist trade in Cordova has been the annual Shorebird Festival[66]. This festival is held in early May, when millions of sandpipers, dunlins, and other shorebirds pass through the area as part of their annual migration pattern. The festival brings birders from far and wide to Cordova, and in recent years has grown into a multi-day event that draws media attention to the town and contributes to "name recognition" for Cordova, while also filling the town's hotels and bed-and-breakfasts and making an important contribution to the local economy.

The Shorebird Festival began in 1990 as a small workshop for Cordova residents, co-sponsored by the Copper River Delta Institute and the Cordova Ranger District of Chugach National Forest. In subsequent years, it grew to include more and more visitors from beyond the local area. In 1992, the Cordova Chamber of Commerce (with assistance from the ranger district) received a rural development grant to conduct planning for future festivals and was able to greatly expand the scope and marketing of the festival. One of the key success factors for the Chamber was its ability to partner with the Anchorage Chapter of the Audubon Society to promote the festival in that metropolitan area. Partnerships with travel providers – including Alaska Airlines and Era Aviation, which provide the crucial air links to the town – made it easier for visitors to reach Cordova and to secure reasonably priced accommodation.

The festival now includes not only bird-watching opportunities (though these are unparalleled and are a major draw), but also community events such as concerts, educational programs, and children's activities. Crucially, the Chamber of Commerce has been mindful of the impact of so much human activity on the shorebirds, and has also taken steps to ensure the continued quality of the event. Visitors are provided with information about birding etiquette, and guides from bird-watching groups travel around to check adherence to the rules and monitor the birds' welfare.

Cordova's experience highlights the importance of local leadership and partnerships, targeted marketing of affinity groups, and careful maintenance of the quality of the visitor experience and the impacts on natural resources. The event's planners, through their partnership efforts, also recognized the importance of affordable and reliable transportation access as an indispensable

---

[66] Material in this section is drawn from the USDA Rural Information Center "Case Studies: Forest-Based Partnership Initiatives," August 1995, and from the Cordova Chamber of Commerce.

part of expanding the festival's reach. Cordova also points out the pros and cons of approaching tourism development through an event- or festival-based approach: the limited duration of the event means that the economic impacts are more limited, but also ensures that tourism does not rapidly change the character of the community in unintended ways.

Northern Forest Heritage Park, Berlin, N.H.

The forests of northern New England have long been recognized as a valuable resource, by Native Americans and immigrant settlers alike, and the area's communities have a long and proud history of involvement in the timber, potash, and paper industries. Like many resource-dependent regions, however, they have felt the effects of shifts in commodity markets and global competition. The region's timber and paper production has been falling for over three decades and the associated economic dislocation has been substantial.

While traditional resource jobs are growing more scarce, there is a recognition that the forest can serve as the linchpin of a more diversified regional economy that includes recreation and tourism as important components. As one local advocate puts it, "We live in the twenty first century. We don't need hemlock bark for tanning; we don't need potash from burning maples. But we need the forest still – need it for hiking trails, need it for locally milled crown moulding, need it for hunting and birdwatching, need it because we are people of the forest."[67]

One component of this effort to diversify the economy while honoring the important role of the forest and the heritage of the region's people is the Northern Forest Heritage Park in Berlin, New Hampshire. The heritage park, which opened in 1994, interprets the social, economic, and ecological history of the "working forest" of the Upper Androscoggin River Valley, with an emphasis on the stories of the immigrant families who worked in the area's logging camps and mills during the late 19th and early 20th centuries. The heart of the park is a full-scale reproduction of a turn-of-the-century logging camp and boarding house, spread out over a three-acre waterfront site, where visitors can learn about these immigrants' experiences. A nearby museum provides further interpretation through a mixture of static and interactive exhibits. The heritage park also hosts special events such as a lumberjack competition and educational programs, and an onsite gift shop specializes in the work of local artists and artisans.

The heritage park, by one calculation, contributed $500,000 to the local economy during the first ten years of its existence. When income in the form of federal grants and other assistance is included, the figure is closer to $2 million.

As with other case studies, the Northern Forest Heritage Park has benefited from its partnerships, which include support from the state government, University of New Hampshire, and local economic development groups. The establishment of a Great North Woods regional tourism organization has also helped to raise tourists' awareness of the opportunities for recreational and educational opportunities in the far northern part of the state. Coordinated planning across different levels of government is also a factor; in 2005, the state of New Hampshire purchased

---

[67] "Shaping the Northern Forest Economy," Northern Forest Alliance, February 2002, foreword by Bill McKibben. Other material in this section comes from Northern Forest Alliance, "Regional Success Stories" and from "Celebrating the Heritage of the North Country," *NH Matters*, Public Service of New Hampshire, February 2003.

land near Berlin to create Jericho Lake State Park, bolstering the visitor potential of the area. The heritage park also capitalizes on the trends toward cultural and heritage tourism; visitors in this segment typically stay longer and spend more than other visitors.

Iceland

Iceland's residents have relied on ocean fishing, particularly for cod and other white fish, for subsistence and trade for centuries. Even today, fish products account for fully 70 percent of the nation's export earnings. This reliance on fishing has made the country vulnerable to changes in fish stocks, world market prices, and international agreements about exclusive economic zones within the North Atlantic. The government of Iceland has therefore pursued a strategy of encouraging a more diverse economic base – of which tourism is one part – as a buffer against these kinds of economic shocks[68].

Iceland, like southeast Alaska, has become a well-known and popular tourist destination despite being perceived as a remote, northern location and despite the time and expense that is required to reach the area from "outside." As in Alaska, one factor in its success has been the ability to trade on that very remoteness as a sign of an unspoiled location offering rewarding experiences. Iceland has also been able to use its geothermal activity and hot springs to create a unique identify and distinguish itself from other Nordic regions.

Transportation has also been an important factor in developing Iceland's tourism – much more directly than in the other cases examined here. The national air carrier, Icelandair, has long offered some of the most inexpensive flights between North America and Europe (for those willing to make a connection in Reykjavik) and has used its pricing structure to encourage these transatlantic air travelers to take a low-cost stopover in Iceland. This laid the groundwork for increasing awareness of Iceland as a tourism destination and brought in visitors who might otherwise have balked at the high cost of traveling to Iceland as a standalone trip. With Iceland more established as a destination in its own right, Icelandair now owns several Reykjavik hotels and sells all-inclusive vacation packages.

Analysis of Iceland's experience has also examined the roles played by national, regional, and local tourism marketing and development agencies. Local and grassroots efforts are deemed to have been most influential in guiding the development of tourist facilities, including a supply of lodging for visitors that was established through a cooperatively run farmhouse accommodation program. The national government provides international marketing but otherwise takes a more hands-off role.

One of the most important lessons from Iceland's experience is that while tourism is a vital and growing industry for the country, it has *complemented* rather than *supplanted* more traditional activities. Many of the visitor-oriented activities are logical outgrowths of resource industries and make use of existing capital, labor, and infrastructure. As an example, local fishermen have developed whale-watching tours as a means of garnering extra seasonal income, using the same

---

[68] Information in this section is drawn from Baum, T. "The decline of the traditional North Atlantic fisheries and tourism's response: the cases of Iceland and Newfoundland," *Current Issues in Tourism*, Vol. 2, No. 1, pp. 47-67, 1999.

boats and crews that would ordinarily be employed in fishing. As Thomas Baum notes, "[In] many Icelandic communities, tourism does not, at present, represent significant new or additional employment although this situation may change if growth continues. Rather, it acts to supplement and support the existing rural or maritime economy – quiet rather than revolutionary diversification."[69]

Nantucket, Mass.

Perhaps the first American community to make the transition from resource-extraction to tourism was Nantucket, Massachusetts. Throughout the 18th and early 19th centuries, Nantucket was one of the most prosperous towns in the nation by virtue of its dominance of the lucrative whaling industry. In the 1840s, however, it was beset by a number of unfavorable developments, notably the growing use of kerosene and other petroleum-based fuels for lighting, which depressed the demand for whale oil and ultimately put an end to the whaling industry altogether. The island also contended with a sandbar that blocked the harbor entrance and with a major fire that destroyed many of the buildings in town.

Economically and socially devastated, islanders nonetheless saw the potential for attracting visitors to Nantucket during the summer – particularly city residents, who were eager, long before the advent of air conditioning, to seek cooler climes and fresh ocean air. As early as 1845, a local newspaper article noted, "A larger number than usual have resorted to the island the present season, in quest of health or pleasure... *If suitable accommodations were provided*, [the island] would take a prominent station among the watering places, which collect their crowds during the summer months" (emphasis added).[70]

By the 1870s, as the idea of a family-oriented "summer vacation" began to take hold among the Victorian middle classes of the east coast, tourism to Nantucket grew substantially. This growth was aided in part by a marketing effort by the town, which circulated a flyer on "Nantucket Island, An Ideal Health and Vacation Resort" and advertised the availability of two daily boat trips from the mainland.[71] In recent years, the development of faster ferries and commuter flights has increased the island's accessibility, and the local tourism industry has worked hard to make Nantucket more of a year-round destination by adding festival weekends to the shoulder-season calendar. Despite the enormous growth in visitation to the island, the architectural character of the town and the natural beauty of the landscape have been largely preserved through landmark designations, strict local land-use planning, and diligent local conservation efforts. Visitors' contributions to motor vehicle traffic and congestion have also been mitigated through an extensive network of bicycle paths, a seasonal bus service, and *de facto* limits on the number of vehicles that are transported from the mainland.

---

[69] Baum, T. "The decline of the traditional North Atlantic fisheries and tourism's response: the cases of Iceland and Newfoundland," *Current Issues in Tourism*, Vol. 2, No. 1, pp. 47-67, 1999.

[70] Nantucket Inquirer, 1845, quoted in Oldham, Elizabeth. "Nantucket in a Nutshell," *Historic Nantucket*, Winter 2000. Nantucket, Mass.: Nantucket Historical Association.

[71] Oldham, Elizabeth. "Nantucket in a Nutshell," *Historic Nantucket*, Winter 2000. Nantucket, Mass.: Nantucket Historical Association.

What is perhaps most instructive about the Nantucket example is that, although the transition to tourism took place largely during a different era, the experience is nonetheless consistent with many of the general principles described in the previous section. These include the development of accommodations matched to visitor needs; effective marketing targeted to a key audience; and conscientious, community-based planning that protects the "authenticity" and quality of the visitor experience. On the question of transportation accessibility, the island has struck a balance between providing convenient access and preserving the "separateness" or "island-ness" that appeals to some vacationers.

Next Steps: Stakeholder Involvement and Tourism Scenarios

This memorandum is the first component in the Tongass National Forest Transportation System Opportunity Study. In the coming months, project staff will begin contacting local stakeholders to gain their perspective on opportunities in the Hoonah and Wrangell ranger districts, and to analyze what the development of these opportunities would mean for the region's transportation network and economy.

At this stage, the available literature on tourism and recreation impacts, combined with a profile of the region, suggests a number of potential options, which are briefly outlined below. It should be stressed that these do not represent specific proposals for attractions or activities at particular sites, since that is properly the role of the local stakeholders themselves. Rather, these options simply represent strategic-level options for marketing the area and planning for visitation.

At the *macro* level, smaller and more remote communities in southeast Alaska will need to consider how to "position" themselves within the tourism and recreation marketplace – that is, what types of visitors they will seek to attract, for how long, and for what sorts of experiences. The answers to these questions depend in part on the types of changes to the look and feel of their community that local people are willing to accept. Some possibilities include:

- Working with the travel industry to become a port of call for some Alaska cruises, thus focusing on accommodating large numbers of day-use visitors;
- Targeting independent travelers interested in local recreational, cultural, and eco-tourism opportunities;
- Micro-targeting of specific affinity groups or overseas markets, based on local assets and ties;
- Developing attractions for shorter-distance travelers, including the local, regional, and in-state Alaska markets; and/or
- Developing a festival or special event (such as the Cordova Shorebird Festival described above) that would periodically bring many visitors to the area for a short period of time.

The *micro* level consists of the specific activities and attractions that would draw visitors. Local stakeholders will have the most insight into which activities are most promising in a particular area, as well as the extent to which the activity would be consistent with local attitudes and priorities. An initial list might include the following:

- Nature observation: birds, bears, fish, whales;
- Wilderness experiences and sports: hiking, camping, trekking, kayaking, skiing, snowshoeing;

- Hunting and fishing;
- Off-road / all-terrain vehicle recreation;
- Heritage tourism: aspects of local culture (both indigenous and European) and industrial history (e.g. cannery); and
- Local arts and crafts.

Obviously, there is a high degree of interdependence between the macro and micro levels: the nature of the local attractions will determine the types of visitors most likely to come and the most appropriate marketing strategy. One of the main goals of a community planning effort is to identify a "good fit" between the macro and micro levels, while also structuring tourism development so that local people can benefit.

Bibliography on Tourism Development: Lessons Learned, Economic Impacts, Transportation, and Case Studies

Addison, L. An Approach to Community-Based Tourism Planning in the Baffin Region, Canada's Far North. A chapter in L.C. Harrison and W. Husbands (Eds.) *Practicing Responsible Tourism: International Case Studies in Tourism Planning, Policy and Development.* New York: John Wiley and Son. 1996.

Aldrich, Lorna and Lorin Kusmin. Rural Economic Development What Makes Rural Communities Grow? United States Department of Agriculture, Agriculture Information Bulletin No. 737, September 1997.

Allen, Stewart D. and Guy Robertson, Julie Schaefers. Economies in Transition: An Assessment of Trends Relevant to Management of the Tongass National Forest. United States Department of Agriculture, Forest Service, Pacific Northwest Research Station, General Technical Report PNW-GTR-417, April 1998

Barnes, Trevor J. and Roger Hayter. 'The Little Town That Did': Flexible Accumulation and Community Response in Chemainus, British Columbia. *Regional Studies.* Volume 26, Number 7 / Pages: 647 – 663. 1992.

Baum, T. The Decline of the Traditional North Atlantic Fisheries and Tourism's Response: The Cases of Iceland and Newfoundland. *Current Issues in Tourism* Vol. 2, No. 1: p. 47-67, 1999.

Bori-Sanz, Monica and Anssi Niskanen. Nature-based Tourism in Forests as a Tool for Rural Development – Analysis of Three Study Areas in North Karelia (Finland), Scotland and the Catalan Pyrenees. European Forest Institute (EFI), Internal Report No. 7, 2002

Bowe, Scott A. and David W. Marcouiller. Natural Resources and the Tourism-Timber Tradeoff: Issues of Regional Dependency and Economic Diversity. Paper for presentation at the 35th Annual Conference of the Mid-continent Regional Science Association held June 3-5, 2004 in Madison, Wisconsin.

Brooks, David J. and Richard W. Haynes. Recreation and Tourism in South-Central Alaska: Synthesis of Recent Trends and Prospects. United States Department of Agriculture, Forest Service, Pacific Northwest Research Station, General Technical Report PNW-GTR-511, August 2001.

Bryson, Connie. Ecotourism: Tourists and Trees in Alberta. *Agriculture and Forestry Bulletin*, Vol. 12, No. 4: pp. 15-16. 1989.

Burr, Steven W. A Conceptual Model for Facilitating Rural Tourism Development. *Proceedings of the 1996 Northeastern Recreation Research Symposium.* U.S. Dept. of Agriculture, Forest Service, Northeastern Forest Experiment Station Report, General Technical Report NE-232, pp. 15-18. 1997.

Cerveny, Lee K. Preliminary Research Findings from a Study of the Sociocultural Effects of Tourism in Haines, Alaska. United States Department of Agriculture, Forest Service, Pacific Northwest Research Station, General Technical Report PNW-GTR-612, July 2004

Crone, Lisa K. Southeast Alaska Economics: A Resource-Abundant Region Competing in a Global Marketplace. *Landscape and Urban Planning.* Vol. 72, p.215-233. 2005

Crone, Lisa K. and Pat Reed, Julie Schaefers. Social and Economic Assessment of the Chugach National Forest Area. United States Department of Agriculture, Forest Service, Pacific Northwest Research Station, General Technical Report PNW-GTR-561, December 2002

Dahms, Fredric. Economic Revitalization in St. Jacobs, Ontario: Ingredients for Transforming a Dying Village into a Thriving Small Town. *Small Town*, Vol. 21, No. 6: pp. 12-18. 1991.

Edgell, David L. and Mary Lynn Cartwright. How One Kansas Town Used Tourism to Revitalize its Economic Base - Fort Scott, Kansas. Business America, Nov 5, 1990

Edgell, David L. Sr. A Small Community Adopts Tourism as a Development Tool - Johnson County, Tennessee. Business America, April 20, 1992

Fairley, Andrew. Adding Value to Local Communities – The Key to Successful Sustainable Tourism. Presented to the 13th PATA Adventure Travel & Ecotourism Conference & Mart Dambulla, Sri Lanka. January 31, 2001

Fay, Ginny, and Kay Brown, Chris Rose. (Prosperous Future Development (PFD) Coalition) An Economic Vision for a Prosperous Alaska. February 29, 2004

Fredrick, M. Rural Tourism and Economic Development. *Economic Development Quarterly* 7:215-224. 1993.

Gartner, William C. Rural Tourism Development in the USA. *International Journal of Tourism Research*. Vol. 6, No. 3: p. 151-164. 2004

Gartner, William C. and Linda J. Limback, Daniel L. Erkkila. Transportation Barriers Affecting International Visitors to Minnesota. Minnesota Department of Transportation Office of Research Services. December 2000.

Gibson, Lay James. The Potential for Tourism Development in Nonmetropolitan Areas. pp. 145-164, in David L. Barkley, ed., *Economic Adaptation*. Boulder, Colorado: Westview Press. 1993.

Guglielmino, J. E. Touring to Economic Health. *American Forests*, Vol. 103, No. 4: p. 31. 1998.

Høyer, Karl G. Sustainable Tourism or Sustainable Mobility? The Norwegian Case. *Journal of Sustainable Tourism*. Vol. 8, No. 2: p. 147-160. 2000

Kenendy, Liam R, ed. Promoting Tourism in Rural America. *Rural Information Center Publication Series (RICPS)*. No. 60. Rural Information Center/National Agricultural Library. April 1998.

Lane, Bernard. Sustainable Rural Tourism Strategies: A Tool for Development and Conservation. *Journal of Sustainable Tourism*, Vol. 2, Nos. 1 & 2 (1994). Reprinted in: *Interamerican Journal of Environment and Tourism*, Vol. 1, Number 1, p. 12-18 (August 2005).

Mafunzwaini, Aluoneswi Elvis and Leon Hugo. Unlocking the Rural Tourism Potential of the Limpopo province of South Africa: Some strategic guidelines. *Development Southern Africa*. Volume 22, Number 2: p. 251-265 / June 2005

Marcouiller, David W. Toward Integrative Tourism Planning in Rural America. Journal of Planning Literature, Vol. 11, No. 3, 337-357, 1997.

Mazza, Rhonda, tech. ed. Economic Growth and Change in Southeast Alaska. U.S. Department of Agriculture, Forest Service, Pacific Northwest Research Station. Gen. Tech. Rep. PNW-GTR-611, 2004.

McGehee, Nancy G. and Kathleen L. Andereck. Factors Predicting Rural Residents' Support of Tourism. *Journal of Travel Research,* Vol. 43, p. 131-140. November 2004

Morford , Shawn and Dave Robinson, Felice Mazzoni, Cleo Corbett, Heidi Schaiberger. Participatory research in rural communities in transition: A case study of the Malaspina-Ucluelet Research Alliance. *BC Journal of Ecosystem Management. Vol. 5, Number 2* p. 39-43. 2004

Oliver, Tove and Tim Jenkins. Sustaining Rural Landscapes: the role of integrated tourism. *Landscape Research.* Volume 28, Number 3: p. 293 – 307, July 2003.

Rockandel, Catherine. The Road from Resource Dependency to Community Sustainability: The Case of Kimberly, British Columbia: 1966-2001. Master's Thesis, Simon Fraser University, 2005

Saarinen, Jarkko. The Regional Economics of Tourism in Northern Finland: The Socio-economic Implications of Recent Tourism Development and Future Possibilities for Regional Development. *Scandinavian Journal of Hospitality and Tourism.* Vol. 3, Number 2 Pages: 91 – 113. December 2003

Siemens, Lynne. Challenges Faced by Rural/Remote Tourism Businesses on Vancouver Island: An Exploratory Study. Presented at the Eleventh Canadian Congress on Leisure Research, May 17 – 20, 2005

Steck, Birgit, ed. Sustainable Tourism as a Development Option: Practical Guide for Local Planners, Developers and Decision Makers. Federal Ministry for Economic Co-operation and Development, Environment Division, Germany. April 1999

Tabor, Jim. Tourism thrives in the Stowe-Smugglers' Notch Region. *Vermont Business Magazine.* Dec 01, 2004. (FindArticles.com. 08 Nov. 2006)

Timothy, Dallen J. Cooperative Tourism Planning in a Developing Destination. *Journal of Sustainable Tourism.* Vol. 6, No.1: p. 52-68, 1998

Tsoumos, Pete and Richard W. Haynes. An Assessment of Growth and Development Paths for Southeast Alaska. United States Department of Agriculture, Forest Service, Pacific Northwest Research Station, General Technical Report PNW-GTR-620, October 2004

Webster, Henry H. and Daniel E. Chappelle and Stephen C. Andrews. Tourism and Forest Products: Twin Resource Sectors for Effective Community Development in the Lake States. Staff Paper Series Number 124, Department of Forest Resources, College of Natural Resources and the Agricultural Experiment Station, University of Minnesota, St. Paul, MN. November 1997

Wilson, Suzanne and Daniel R. Fesenmaier, Julie Fesenmaier, John C. Van Es. Factors for Success in Rural Tourism Development. *Journal of Travel Research,* Vol. 40, Pages 132-138. November 2001

Appendix B – Stakeholder Contact Plan / Discussion Guide

- **US Forest Service - Ranger Districts – Hoonah & Wrangell**

1. Overview of area
2. Roads and other transportation infrastructure: existing conditions, access management, existing and future plans and projects
3. Community concerns and major stakeholder groups
4. Recreation and tourism: existing patterns and potential development opportunities

- **Government tourism offices**
   - Hoonah, Wrangell municipal governments
   - Alaska DCED

1. Community profiles and current issues
2. Current tourism situation
3. Existing policies, plans, and projects
4. Constraints and community issues
5. Best opportunities for recreation/tourism development and associated transportation issues

- **Tribal governments and corporations**
   - Hoonah Indian Association
   - Huna Totem
   - Wrangell Cooperative Association
   - Central Council Tlingit and Haida
   - Southeast Tribal DOT

1. Status and scope of responsibilities (geographic & functional)
2. Current planned future tourism and recreational areas and opportunities
3. Community issues and constraints
4. Best opportunities and associated transportation issues

- **Convention and visitors bureaus / business groups**
   - Wrangell C&VB
   - Wrangell Chamber of Commerce
   - Hoonah Economic Development Committee

1. Statistics on visitation: counts, visitor profiles and spending data, main attractions, seasonality, recent trends and developments
2. Current plans and projects
3. Constraints and community issues
4. Best opportunities and associated transportation issues

- Recreational and Environmental groups
  - o Southeast Alaska Conservation Council
  - o Sierra Club
  - o Sitka Conservation Society

1. Background on group: goals, history and current projects, membership, geographic scope, relationship with municipal governments and Forest Service
2. Long-term vision for region and viewpoint on local tourism and recreation, including environmental impacts
3. Viewpoints on transportation
4. Effects of increased visitation; more and less sensitive areas
5. Best opportunities and associated transportation issues

- Tour and cruise operators / hospitality industry
- Icy Strait Point
- Tour operators and major hospitality businesses as identified by District Ranger
- Hunting and sport-fishing outfitters/ guides as identified by District Ranger

1. Background on operations: types tours/packages/cruises/services offered, geographic scope, thematic focus, business model, seasonality
2. Visitor profiles and demographics; visitor "psychology"
3. Capacity constraints (internal or external)
4. Current transportation issues
5. Future desired destinations or suggested opportunities, with associated transportation implications

Appendix C – List of Stakeholder-Generated Concepts for Recreation and Tourism Development

Ranger District	Area	Concept
Hoonah, Wrangell		"Milepost"-type guide for Tongass NF / Southeast AK to improve visitor awareness of travel conditions, attractions, amenities, and what to expect
Hoonah, Wrangell		Web-based itinerary planner for independent travelers to improve information and access. Could be combined with Milepost guide and/or an "intermodal transport pass" for travelers (akin to European rail passes).
Hoonah, Wrangell		Expanded SEAtrails efforts: marketing, wayfinding, etc., in conjunction with additional amenities for kayakers (safe havens, tent platforms)
Hoonah, Wrangell		There may be common goals between Central Council Tlingit & Haida. FS, Community programs. Coordinate on their stakeholder communication and regional economic development strategy.
Hoonah, Wrangell		Assess options for "academic recreation," distance learning and field research programs and "virtual reality" visitor experiences
Wrangell	Wrangell Is.	Extend existing 5-mi Zimovia Hwy bike trail; identify areas for additional bike trails and 3-sided shelters
Wrangell	Wrangell Is.	Extend roads to proposed ferry terminal at Fools Inlet
Wrangell	Wrangell Is.	New cabin on road system in partnership with local snowmachine club.
Wrangell	Wrangell Is. & mainland	Improved access to alpine and sub-alpine areas
Wrangell	Wrangell Is.	Construct additional 1 mile road segment to link two road systems and create a full "loop" through town
Wrangell	Anan Creek	Improve dock at Anan to allow wider range of visitors to access
Wrangell	Several locations	Partner with Alaska Crossings program on formalizing portage trails (Etolin Is. - Anita Bay and Portage Bay on south Mitkof Is.) and improving access to ridges and high terrain
Wrangell	City of Wrangell	Use high-speed telecom lines to promote tele-work, tele-medicine in Wrangell
Wrangell	City of Wrangell	Partner with Nolan Center / museum to draw cultural tourists, conventions, Elderhostel groups, conventions
Wrangell	Wrangell Is.	Create more sheltered picnic and viewing areas for groups, with a reservation system
Wrangell	Wrangell Is.	Assist with Pat's Lake project
Wrangell	Wrangell Is.	Finish building campground areas

Ranger District	Area	Concept
Wrangell	Wrangell Is.	Build skateboard park
Wrangell	City of Wrangell	Partner with Muskeg Meadows golf course to draw independent travelers; possibility for package tours or network of courses in SE Alaska
Wrangell	S. Mitkof Is.	Dredging and improvements to Banana Point launch area (used by outfitters & local travelers)
Wrangell	Wrangell Is.	Develop network of ski-in, ski-out cabins or yurts to promote winter recreation
Hoonah	Chichagof Is.	Widen road for safety of bus tours, and add bike path on route from port to Spasski area
Hoonah	Chichagof Is.	Identify overgrown roads suitable for ATV tours
Hoonah	Chichagof Is.	Partner with HIA to declare Tribal road system to achieve road improvements
Hoonah	Chichagof Is.	Partner with HIA on projects including interpretive signage; walk/hike/bike trails; access to headlands and historical Blood Painting
Hoonah	City of Pelican	Improve trails leading from town
Hoonah	Hoonah / Gustavus / Glacier Bay	Improve ferry service and schedules between Hoonah and Gustavus: Hoonah residents would gain improved access to Glacier Bay and park visitors would have the opportunity to day-trip to Hoonah.
Hoonah	Gustavus / Glacier Bay	Promote birdwatching in partnership with the many retired naturalists in town
Hoonah	Several locations	Make the USFS permit process for outfitters more user-friendly
Hoonah	Chichagof Is.	Connect the Hoonah road system to the Tenakee Springs road
Hoonah	Chichagof Is.	Formalize some rough bear-viewing trails used by outfitters. Maintenance can be done in partnership.
Hoonah	Chichagof Is.	Construct boat haul-outs at Freshwater Bay, False Creek
Hoonah	Several locations	Construct more USFS cabins; HRD has fewer cabins than other districts
Hoonah	Freshwater Bay	Make better use of this area, which has existing water/sewer hookups and potential for more shelters and marine access
Hoonah	City of Hoonah	Develop a hub-and-spoke ferry system centered on Hoonah, improving access for nearby smaller communities such as Elfin Cove, Pelican, and eliminating need to go into Juneau to change boats
Hoonah	Chichagof Is.	Increase lodging options on-island for independent travelers. Possibility of converting under-used or un-used USFS buildings to commercial accommodation.
Hoonah	City of Hoonah	Electric inter-tie project to Juneau

Ranger District	Area	Concept
Hoonah	City of Hoonah	Potential for the incorporation of a "Glacier Bay" or "Northern Southeast" borough government with road authority
Hoonah	Hoonah / Whitestone Harbor	Assess options for shuttle transit service: visitor access to Whitestone and mobility for residents of housing project
Hoonah	Icy Strait Pt / Hoonah	Safety improvements to walking path between downtown and cruise ship area
Hoonah	Icy Strait Pt / Hoonah	Assess feasibility of stocking fish ponds near Icy Strait for cruise visitor fishing experience

www.ingramcontent.com/pod-product-compliance
Lightning Source LLC
Chambersburg PA
CBHW080425290526
45791CB00008BA/2408